SpringerBriefs in Ethics

Springer Briefs in Ethics envisions a series of short publications in areas such as business ethics, bioethics, science and engineering ethics, food and agricultural ethics, environmental ethics, human rights and the like. The intention is to present concise summaries of cutting-edge research and practical applications across a wide spectrum.

Springer Briefs in Ethics are seen as complementing monographs and journal articles with compact volumes of 50 to 125 pages, covering a wide range of content from professional to academic. Typical topics might include:

- Timely reports on state-of-the art analytical techniques
- A bridge between new research results, as published in journal articles, and a contextual literature review
- A snapshot of a hot or emerging topic
- In-depth case studies or clinical examples Presentations of core concepts that students must understand in order to make independent contributions

Motsamai Molefe

An Introduction to Human Rights in African Philosophy

Springer

Motsamai Molefe
Graduate School of Business Leadership
University of South Africa
Pretoria, South Africa

ISSN 2211-8101 ISSN 2211-811X (electronic)
SpringerBriefs in Ethics
ISBN 978-3-032-04446-4 ISBN 978-3-032-04447-1 (eBook)
https://doi.org/10.1007/978-3-032-04447-1

This Springer imprint is published by the registered company Springer Nature Switzerland AG
The registered company address is: Gewerbestrasse 11, 6330 Cham, Switzerland

"Motsamai Molefe's latest book provides an accurate and thoughtful critical discussion of positions on human rights salient in contemporary African philosophy. Including discussion of related concepts such as personhood and dignity, the overview will be of clear interest not only to philosophers, but also to those in cognate disciplines such as normative sociology, political theory, international relations, and law".

—Thaddeus Metz, *Research Professor of Philosophy, University of Pretoria*

"The book is a groundbreaking introductory exploration of some of the core ideas about human rights from an African perspective. Indeed, Motsamai Molefe's incisive analysis offers a nuanced and thoughtful examination of some of the leading theories in the field. This book is a must-read for anyone interested in human rights, African philosophy and the pursuit of justice".

—Aribiah David Attoe, *Lecturer of Philosophy, University of the Witwatersrand*

Preface

This book, *A Short Introduction to Human Rights in African Philosophy*, is born from a deep-seated conviction: to contribute meaningfully to the burgeoning field of African philosophy. Specifically, its aim is to enrich the discourse surrounding human rights by grounding it firmly within the rich and diverse intellectual traditions of the African continent. For too long, conversations about human rights have predominantly been shaped by Western philosophical frameworks. This work seeks to demonstrate the profound insights and unique perspectives that African philosophy offers on the fundamental questions of dignity, justice, community, and individual flourishing, thereby expanding and globalizing our understanding of human rights. It is an invitation to recognize and engage with the vital contributions of African thought to this universal subject.

The journey towards this book has been a long and winding one, born from a persistent observation: despite the growing richness of African philosophical discourse, there remained a conspicuous absence of dedicated book-length works on human rights in African philosophy. This became particularly evident during my initial engagements with the subject. In 2018, I had the privilege of co-editing a special issue titled 'African Philosophy and Human Rights' with my esteemed colleague, Christopher Allsobrook. This endeavour attracted meaningful contributions from leading scholars of African thought, offering diverse perspectives on the intersection of these critical areas. While the special issue was well-received, I remained acutely aware that it was only a partial step; a comprehensive, accessible introduction to the subject in book form was still sorely needed.

This enduring need prompted an earlier, albeit slightly deviated, attempt: the writing of *Human Rights in African Philosophy: A Very Short Introduction*. While that book served its purpose, the ongoing reflections from various scholars in African philosophy, though not in the form of dedicated volumes, continued to underscore the gap. The urgency was further amplified in 2023 when, once again, I co-edited a significant volume with Christopher Allsobrook, this time focusing on 'Human Dignity in an African Context'. This deep dive into human dignity further emphasized the intrinsic link between dignity and human rights, highlighting the critical necessity for a focused work on human rights itself. It became clear that an introductory book that could serve as a valuable resource for both scholars within African philosophy and those from other philosophical traditions was not just desirable, but essential. This current book, therefore, was born out of this persistent intellectual vacuum and a strong desire to provide that much-needed introduction.

It is with a profound sense of sadness and a deep reverence that I acknowledge the passing of three intellectual giants whose pioneering work laid much of the groundwork for contemporary African philosophy: *Professor Ifeanyi Menkiti*, *Professor Kwasi Wiredu*, and *Professor Kwame Gyekye*. These remarkable thinkers were among the leading pioneers who profoundly influenced my own philosophical thinking and approach. Their rigorous analyses, their steadfast commitment to intellectual integrity, and their innovative engagements with both indigenous African thought and global philosophical traditions continue to shape much of the arguments and perspectives presented within these pages. This book hails them as true heroes of African philosophy, whose intellectual torch continues to illuminate the path forward for Africa as it strives to make an indelible contribution to global thought. Their legacies serve as a constant reminder of the depth and resilience of African philosophical inquiry.

This book consciously places the insightful voices of African scholars and those deeply engaged with African philosophical traditions at the forefront of the discussion. By centring the work of thinkers such as *Ifeanyi Menkiti, Kwame Gyekye, Polycarp Ikuenobe, Thaddeus Metz,* and *Christopher Allsobrook*, this text aims not only to amplify their significant contributions to political philosophy within an African context but also to extend a sincere invitation. It is an invitation to scholars from other philosophical traditions worldwide—be they Western, Eastern, or otherwise—to engage with, learn from, and critically reflect upon the leading thinkers of political philosophy in African thought. The richness of these perspectives, often overlooked in mainstream global philosophical discourse, offers fertile ground for comparative analysis and mutual intellectual enrichment.

Ultimately, this book serves as a foundational step. While it delves into the essential aspects of human rights from an African philosophical lens, it also envisions future explorations. It is my hope that this book will lay the groundwork for another, more extensive work that will take a deeply comparative approach, examining the convergences and divergences between African philosophical perspectives on human rights and those from other global traditions. Such a comparative undertaking, I believe, will further solidify the place of African philosophy as an indispensable voice in the ongoing, worldwide dialogue on human rights.

Pretoria, South Africa Motsamai Molefe

Acknowledgements

Writing a book is a journey fraught with challenges and triumphs, demanding not only intellectual rigour but also profound resilience and unwavering belief. As I reflect on the completion of this manuscript, my heart overflows with an immense sense of gratitude towards the numerous individuals and institutions who have, directly and indirectly, shaped its very essence and brought it to fruition. Their support, guidance, and encouragement have been the steadfast anchors that kept me grounded, the gentle winds that propelled me forward, and the illuminating lights that guided my path through moments of both clarity and uncertainty. This work, in many ways, is as much a testament to their unwavering faith in me as it is to my own persistent efforts.

This book is dedicated to the enduring legacies of the late *Professor Kwasi Wiredu* and *Professor Ifeanyi Menkiti*. Their groundbreaking contributions to African philosophy and their profound insights into the nature of personhood, community, and knowledge have been a constant source of inspiration and intellectual guidance. Their work has not only illuminated the rich philosophical traditions of Africa but has also challenged universal philosophical discourse to engage more deeply with diverse perspectives. It is my sincere hope that this manuscript, in some small way, honours their pioneering spirit and continues the vital conversations they so passionately advanced.

Foremost, I must offer my most profound gratitude to the Almighty God, the source of all wisdom, strength, and blessings. Every breath I take, every thought I conceive, and every word I pen is a gift from His divine grace. His unfailing love has been my constant companion, providing solace in times of doubt and inspiration in moments of creative void. It is through His boundless mercy that I have been granted the intellect, the perseverance, and the opportunities to embark on this academic journey and see it through to its completion. This accomplishment is, first and foremost, a testament to His magnificent providence and a humble offering of thanks for the countless blessings bestowed upon my life, far beyond what I could ever articulate. Without His guiding hand, this endeavour would have remained but a distant dream.

My deepest appreciation is extended to the *UNISA School of Business Leadership*. This institution has been more than just an academic environment; it has been a crucible of intellectual growth, a beacon of knowledge, and a nurturing ground for critical thought. The resources, the stimulating discussions, and the robust academic framework provided by the SBL have been instrumental in shaping my research and refining my perspectives. The vibrant academic community within its halls fosters an environment where ideas are challenged, debated, and ultimately strengthened, and for that, I am eternally thankful. The SBL's commitment to academic excellence and its supportive infrastructure have undeniably played a pivotal role in enabling the rigorous inquiry that underpins this book.

To *Professor Pumela Msweli*, I extend a special, heartfelt thank you that words can scarcely encompass. Professor Msweli, your unwavering belief in my capabilities, even when my own conviction faltered, has been a source of immeasurable strength and motivation. Your mentorship transcended mere academic guidance; it was a profound act of faith that nurtured my intellectual spirit and encouraged me to push beyond perceived limitations. Your constant encouragement, insightful critiques, and the profound trust you placed in my vision for this project provided the scaffolding upon which this entire work was built. Your influence has been truly transformative, and for your profound impact on my academic and personal journey, I am deeply, genuinely grateful.

This work stands on the shoulders of giants, and I am profoundly indebted to the vibrant *community of intellectuals* who have not only influenced but continue to influence my work as a philosopher. From foundational texts that ignited my initial curiosity to contemporary debates that sharpen my arguments, the intellectual tapestry woven by these thinkers has been a constant source of inspiration and challenge. Their ideas have shaped my understanding of the world, broadened my horizons, and provided the critical tools necessary for deep philosophical inquiry. This ongoing engagement with diverse perspectives continually enriches my intellectual landscape and informs the very core of my philosophical explorations.

I wish to express immense gratitude to *Professor Thaddeus Metz* and *Professor Christopher Allsobrook* for their invaluable participation in the workshop dedicated to this manuscript. Their willingness to engage deeply with the material, their incisive comments, and their profound wisdom were truly appreciated. The critiques and insights they offered during those sessions were not just helpful; they were transformative, prompting me to reconsider, refine, and strengthen various arguments within these pages. Their intellectual generosity and constructive feedback have undoubtedly elevated the quality and coherence of this book, and for their significant contribution, I am profoundly thankful.

Finally, and perhaps most importantly, my heartfelt thanks go to the extraordinary *community of friends* who continue to believe in me and support me through thick and thin. Their unwavering friendship has been a source of comfort, laughter, and profound encouragement. They are the silent pillars of strength who have celebrated my small victories, offered a listening ear during moments of frustration, and reminded me of the broader purpose of this journey. To *Tumelo Mohotlane, Dumisane Mbanyela, Sizwe Koom, Xolani Msimango, Promise Aphana, Sihle*

Khanyile, Akhona Mafani, Siyabonga Makwethu, Mr Joko, and *Majikela*—your loyalty, your companionship, and your belief in my dreams mean more to me than words can express. This book is as much a reflection of your steadfast support as it is of my own efforts. Thank you for being the incredible individuals you are, and for making this journey infinitely richer and more meaningful.

This book is the culmination of years of dedication, but it is also a testament to the power of collaboration, mentorship, and unwavering support. To everyone who has played a part, no matter how small, in bringing this vision to fruition, please accept my sincerest and deepest thanks.

Competing Interests The author has no competing interests to declare that are relevant to the content of this manuscript.

Contents

Chapter 1
Introduction to Human Rights in African Philosophy

Introduction

This book contributes to ongoing conversations and debates on human rights in philosophy. It aims to contribute to the discourse on human rights, drawing from the African philosophical perspective. Roughly, the concept of 'human rights' refers to special moral claims (or entitlements) that moral agents or citizens can make against their governments and fellow citizens (Feinberg 1971; Donnelly 1982). Human rights, as special claims or entitlements, generally imagine (or impose) a relationship between the right-holder and the one whom the right creates a duty for, the state or individuals—the relationship between the right-holder and the duty-bearer (Donnelly 2009). Human rights serve as the core of political morality or social justice in modern political thought and practice across the world. They serve as the standard for the "decent treatment of people by the government" (Waldron 1987). A good government espouses, protects and promotes the human rights of its citizens.

Indeed, modern political thought, particularly since the adoption of the Universal Declaration of Human Rights in 1948, tends to frame social justice, a just government, and a good society in terms of human rights. In the contemporary global landscape, human rights symbolize the promise of civilization, peace, and prosperity among nations. Historically, the idea of human rights emerged in the Global North (Donnelly 2009). The modern concept of human rights has deep historical and philosophical roots that go back centuries in the Euro-American context, but it became significant and relevant due to the devastating conflicts of the twentieth century. Before the Second World War, ideas associated with human rights tended to be very narrow in that they did not have a universal approach—human rights were usually limited to national citizenship or specific legal frameworks. This narrow focus and scope of human rights tended to leave individuals vulnerable to their own governments.

M. Molefe, *An Introduction to Human Rights in African Philosophy*, SpringerBriefs in Ethics, https://doi.org/10.1007/978-3-032-04447-1_1

The large-scale horrors and humiliation that occurred during the war horrors and the scale of atrocities witnessed during the war, particularly the holocaust, reveal in the most concerning form the dangers of unbridled state power and the degradation of human populations (Habermas 2010). The deliberate annihilation of millions of people on the basis of bigotries rooted in tribalism, ethnicity, race, and religion, among others, demonstrated the crucial need to recognize and protect human dignity (Hughes 2011). The international community reacted to the moral crisis by forming the United Nations in 1945, which subsequently developed the universal moral-legal-political code—Universal Declaration of Human Rights (UNDR)—that served as a beacon of a new world order grounded on recognizing human dignity and protecting it via the protocol of human rights (Donnelly 1982). The aim of the UNDR was to ensure a global society based on a universal framework for peace, stability and justice.

The dominant debates in the literature on human dignity and human rights in the aftermath of the UNDR tend to reflect the moral-political assumptions, ethos and aspirations of the Global North (Donnelly 2009). Though initially, the idea of human rights was influential in the global north, its influence has since spread to almost all the corners of the globe (Donnelly 1982, 2009). This fact is borne out by the fact that most countries are signatories to the Universal Declaration of Human Rights (Rosen 2012). Moreover, the constitutions of many countries tend to consider rights to be a central kernel for imagining social justice. In the contemporary world, human rights are a token and promise of civilization, peace, and prosperity among nations (Hughes 2011). Whereas conversations on human rights tend to emerge from the Euro-American contexts characterized by the axiological and cultural assumptions of those communities, this book engages conversations and debates on human rights from an African perspective. I use the idea of 'African perspective' to refer almost exclusively to the literature on human rights in the tradition of African philosophy.

Two considerations concerning the literature on human rights motivate the emergence of this book. First, as already noted, much of the literature on human rights tends to emerge from the intellectual traditions in the global north, particularly from the Euro-American contexts, experiences and practices (Griffin 2008; Beitz 2009; Hopgood et al. 2017; Freeman 2022). Moreover, this literature on human rights usually focuses almost entirely on the Euro-American cultures and the axiological assumptions embedded in them, as if they are representative of the whole human situation and experience (which is not true). Often, this literature tends to ignore or exclude emerging or marginal perspectives from Africa, among others. As much as the Euro-American philosophical contribution is an important and integral part of the conversations on human rights, there is no denying that it is also characterized by concerning elements.

For the most part, conversations and debates on human rights take place in the context of a cultural monologue, where the voices, perspectives, cultural, political, and axiological assumptions from the Euro-American context become the defining features of human rights. The category *human*, ontologically and otherwise, goes beyond the Euro-American context; it is diverse, complex, and dynamic embracing a multiplicity of cultures. If human rights are genuinely *human* rights and they are about all of us human beings on this planet, it should follow then that the scope of human experiences, voices, perspectives, cultural, political, and axiological assumptions must of necessity go beyond the Euro-American geography to include other parts of the world, such as Asia and Africa.

Undoubtedly, African and Asian cultures, among others, do have intellectual resources and worldviews that can express and expand our conceptions of human rights. Some scholars of African thought have aptly expressed concern regarding the dominance of the Euro-American perspective on human rights. For example, Anke Graness (2015: 126) makes several observations about the status of the literature on the debates on global justice (or global ethics). First, she observes that the literature on global ethics is not global in as far as it is dominated by scholars from the Global North. Second, and related to the first concern, the cultural assumptions, and the axiological frameworks tend to take the shape of the Euro-American cultural structures. Finally, she argues that a debate on global justice would truly be global if it is characterized by an "intercultural, interreligious, and international exchange of ideas". In the same vein, commenting on the literature on global justice in the discipline of philosophy, Jonathan Chimakonam (2017: 120) observes that the debate on global justice is dominated by Euro-American scholars in the discipline of philosophy and it tends to exclude contributions from African philosophy. He concludes by observing that the exclusion and marginalization of African philosophy is an instance of epistemic injustice, which impoverishes rather than engages a truly global conversation on issues that affect global humanity (Fricker 2007).

The two scholars of African thought make important observations about global justice. On the one hand, they lament the dominance of the global north's perspectives on major themes affecting all people, such as global justice. The concern points to a particular culture and perspective from some region(s) that pretends to be an 'international' perspective. On the other hand, there is a concern about epistemic injustice, where voices, perspectives, and contributions from other cultures and regions are ignored and marginalized in conversations in which they ought to ordinarily feature (Fricker 2007). These scholars are urging us to consider taking seriously the call for a truly intercultural and global conversation on themes such as social justice, which will involve expanding the table to accommodate all cultural and regional voices and perspectives on crucial human issues.

The dominance of the Euro-American voices and views is not welcome on such pressing human issues as human rights, and it will not help the world in truly pursuing global justice. This is the case because Europe and America have a brutal history of plunder, colonization, slavery, deculturization, and dehumanization in relation to Africa (Biko 2004). The brutal history did not only affect the cultural and economic domains; it also extended to the epistemic domains, where the experiences, ways of knowing, and interpreting the world were erased, marginalized, and generally ignored—epistemic-ide (Mudimbe 1988; Ramose 2009). The call from these scholars of African thought for a genuinely global conversation is an urgent and important one, which requires all of us to give up our bigotry and myopia and embrace the world, its diverse and complex cultures, as a point of departure when engaging on themes like social justice.

Suppose I am correct that human rights are an essential part of social justice. In that case, it seems urgent that we also include perspectives from other parts of the world in our philosophical engagements on human rights, such as the African perspective. This book emerges precisely to respond to the dominance of the Euro-American perspectives on human rights. Alternatively, it considers itself part of the positive response to the call by scholars of African thought that we need to contribute towards creating truly global conversations on human issues like social justice, human dignity, human rights, and so on. The book's aim, motivated by the desire to contribute towards a global conversation on human rights, involves giving the international audience a picture of the concept and debates on human rights anchored on African thought. This aim involves intentionally providing a platform for intellectuals from and those working in African thought, where their intellectual contributions become a guiding light on the concept, conversations, and debates on human rights.

The book aims to construct the engagement on human rights from an African vantage point. In other words, the book's focus will be mainly on voices and perspectives in and from Africa concerning human rights. There is no suggestion that the book will not engage the ideas and arguments of scholars from other traditions of philosophy except that they will not be a major source of intellectual orientation and direction. The overall orientation of the book pivots on constructing a philosophical picture of human rights in African thought, drawing mainly from scholars working in this tradition of philosophy. Hence, this book does not take a cross-cultural or comparative approach to human rights engagements. Instead, it aims to identify and recognize an African perspective and to give it the attention it deserves on human rights. Let the world hear what Africans have to say on this vital topic.

Perhaps, subsequently, in other book projects, I, or any other scholar from the marginal perspective(s), may contribute further to the conversations on human rights by pursuing a more intercultural and comparative approach to human rights. As far as I am aware, there is no monograph dedicated to the subject of human rights in African philosophy. It is this observation or status of affairs in the literature on human rights, both in the African and Euro-American context, which informs and justifies why I exclusively pursue this subject in light of African thought. Hence, a book introducing debates on human rights in African philosophy is urgent and welcome. This book will focus on the theorization of human rights from scholars of African philosophy.

The second consideration that informs the emergence of this book is the status of the literature on human rights in African philosophy. A brief survey of the literature on human rights will expose the reader to more than a dozen academic essays and book chapters on human rights in African philosophy (Cobbah 1987; Menkiti 1984, 2004, 2017; Ake 1987; Gyekye 1997; Ilesamni 2001; Deng 2004; Metz 2012; Oyowe 2014; Ikuenobe 2018; Molefe 2018). These essays provide some of the most valuable insights on human rights from an African perspective. A book dedicated to human rights will be a welcome addition to this literature on human rights, and it will also be a great way to grow the literature on African philosophy.[1] There is no contemporary book in African philosophy that one can use as a useful guide on the concept, conversations, and debates on human rights other than the essays and book chapters scattered everywhere in the literature. This book emerges precisely to close this gap by providing a book on human rights from an African perspective. I believe it will be useful and helpful in the literature for both African and non-African scholars to have a book dedicated to human rights from an African perspective.

I imagine this book not as one that aims to settle major debates in the literature on African philosophy. No. The aim is to present a book that will serve as an introduction to human rights in African philosophy. The book will provide the reader, graduate students, experts in African philosophy, and experts working outside of the tradition of African philosophy who are interested in the African perspective, a general guide on the leading scholars, themes, and debates on human rights in this tradition. I describe the book as an *Introduction* to emphasize that (a) it is not meant to settle or exhaust debates on African philosophy on human rights. Instead, it will identify leading thinkers and theories on human rights in African philosophy. Moreover, (b) the book will not take an argumentative posture. Instead, it will take an expository posture, philosophically clarifying concepts and debates on human rights to give the reader a sense of the status of the debates and major themes in the discussions in the tradition of African philosophy. In other words, the book will not defend a specific view of human rights in African philosophy. At best, it aims to offer a philosophical exposition that will give the reader a sense of the status of the conversations and debates in African philosophy on human rights.

In short, as part of expounding the reasons that justify the emergence of this book in philosophy, I also outlined the book's aims. The book has two aims. First, its primary aim involves adding an African perspective to the debates on human rights, which, as things stand, is dominated by scholars and theories from the Euro-American perspective. Secondly, the book notes the absence of a monograph dedicated to human rights in the tradition of African philosophy. In the quest to grow African philosophy, particularly in the domains of ethical and political theory, this book may be the first (monograph) of its kind to provide an overview or introduction at a conceptual and theoretical level regarding human rights from an African vantage point.

---

[1] I make this claim aware that there is a collected volume 'Human Rights in Africa: Cross Cultural Perspective' that focuses on human rights in African philosophy. This volume is no longer in print and is hardly available. It is also worth noting, however, that of scholars writing on human rights do not tend to cite it, or make reference to it. This is not to say it has nothing to contribute, but it is crucial to note that it has not had an appreciable impact on the debates on human rights in the literature in African philosophy, and globally. The closest that comes to the most recent contribution to human rights in contemporary African philosophy, is a special issue co-edited by myself and Christopher Allsobrook (https://www.berghahnjournals.com/view/journals/theoria/65/157/theoria.65.issue-157.xml). Moreover, this book is different in that it does not take a cross-cultural perspective. Instead, it offers an African cultural and axiological exposition of human rights. Though I believe that cross-cultural comparisons are crucial, I do believe that that an introductory text on human rights in African philosophy should be the starting point.

This chapter provides a bird's-eye view of the issues on human rights in African philosophy. The chapter will proceed as follows. First, it will discuss major themes and debates concerning human rights in African philosophy. Here, I will outline what I consider salient theories of human rights in African philosophy. Second, it will engage the methodological issues of the book. It will specifically focus on two methodological issues: (a) it will provide clarification regarding the use of the concept of 'Africa' when we talk of '*African* philosophy' or '*African* conceptions of human rights', and (b) it will also specify and explain the method the book will use to engage in the conversations and debates on human rights. Finally, we will conclude by discussing the structure of the book.

The Major Themes and Debates on Human Rights in African Philosophy

There have been continuing debates on the concept of human rights in African philosophy. To the best of my knowledge, the first and now out-of-print edited volume 'Human Rights in Africa: A Cross-Cultural Perspective' opened the conversation on human rights (An-Na'im and Deng 1990). The distinctive feature of this volume is that it is intended to be a cross-cultural perspective on human rights, mainly drawn from African scholars. It is worth noting, however, that this volume has not had much impact on the debates on human rights. For example, the influential debate on human rights in African philosophy (between Ifeanyi Menkiti and Kwame Gyekye that has shaped the debates in African philosophy) has not drawn much from this book. The source of the contemporary debates on human rights in African philosophy is traceable to Ifeanyi Menkiti's (1984) influential essay 'Person and Community in African Traditional Thought'.

Two ideas associated with Menkiti animated and steered the entire debate on human rights. On the one hand, his conception of African personhood has been pivotal in debates on moral and political philosophy. The reader will realize throughout the book that the scholars that will be the focus of this book all tend to make their point of departure from Menkiti's conception of personhood, in one way or another. On the other hand, Menkiti's claim that human rights occupy a secondary status in African political theory also animated and directed debates in African philosophy about their relevance and place in this tradition. Three central questions are at the heart of this debate. Is there a relationship between African conceptions of personhood and political theory, particularly concerning human rights? Do human rights have a place in Afro-communitarianism? If they do, what position do they occupy—do human rights occupy a primary or secondary status?

The distinctive feature of these debates on human rights in African philosophy is that they tend to pivot on the African conception of personhood (Ikuenobe 2017a; Allsobrook 2023). Moreover, the conversation seems to proceed on the basis of the assumption that there is a relationship between a conception of a person and a good society (or socially just political arrangements for the purpose of a decent human existence). Gyekye (1992: 102) is explicit regarding this relationship; he avers, "The type of social structure or arrangement evolved by a particular society seems to reflect—and be influenced by—the public conceptions of personhood held in that society." The claim seems to imply that one can derive a political theory from a conception of personhood. In fact, the major debates on human rights in African philosophy have pivoted on contestations concerning personhood and its implications for a proper socio-political order.

The concept of personhood is not absent of its own ambiguities and contestations in the literature on African philosophy (see Kaphagawani 2004; Masolo 2010; Ikuenobe 2017a). The dominant views on human rights differ and depart from a particular conception of personhood; at least this is one common way to read matters in the literature in African philosophy. The reader will notice that the five theories of human rights that will be the focus of this book operate with a particular interpretation or relationship to the concept of personhood and the implication it has for human dignity and human rights.

I divide the debates on human rights into two clusters: the *classical* and *contemporary* theories of human rights in African philosophy. I describe the first cluster as 'classical' as these were among the pioneering contributions to human rights in African philosophy. Specifically, we have the influential debate between the so-called radical and moderate communitarians. Radical communitarianism is associated with John Mbiti, Claudius Ake, and Ifeanyi Menkiti, among others (Gyekye 1992). These scholars advance a particular conception of a person that entails a social structure that places primacy on duties and considers rights secondary in political thought. In this view, a good society or government is defined by exercising duties that promote the common good (Ake 1987). In sum, the importance of a socially oriented conception of a person imagines a duty-based political theory, where rights are secondary. Menkiti is the most influential figure from which we will philosophically explore radical communitarianism.

Moderate communitarianism is another influential classical political theory of rights in African philosophy (Gyekye 1997; Chemhuru 2018). Kwame Gyekye propounds moderate communitarianism as a response and criticism of Menkiti's radical communitarianism. Gyekye's moderate communitarianism disputes Menkiti's radical communitarianism on several crucial points. Mainly, he observes that Menkiti's view on personhood is untenable since it fails to recognise crucial individualistic features of the human person like her autonomy and dignity (Gyekye 1992). He also observes that it fails to correctly identify human rights' relevance, place, and importance in African political theory. Moderate communitarianism promises a political theory that equally prizes duties and rights, and it assigns them equal status. On this view, a plausible conception of a good society involves the state (and its agents) promoting the common good and protecting human dignity. The state promotes the common good via the exercise of duties directed towards addressing human needs or improving the quality of life. The state protects human dignity through the provision of human rights, designed to deliver freedom and equality to all citizens in society.

Menkiti's and Gyekye's contributions to personhood and human rights have significantly shaped the conversations and debates on human rights. This book serves as an introduction to human rights, it approaches the subject in light of the Menkiti-Gyekye debate in African philosophy. The engagements on human rights, however, progressed beyond the debate between radical and moderate communitarianism, to propose novel conceptions of human rights. Under the rubric of *contemporary* conceptions of human rights in African philosophy, I identify at least three salient theories of human rights. First, I consider the friendliness conception of human rights in African philosophy (Metz 2011, 2012). The friendliness view of human rights operates on a moral status approach to human rights (see Toscano 2011).[2] To have moral status, which term in some interpretations may be used interchangeably with human dignity, secures human rights. Human beings have moral status in virtue of possessing the capacity for friendliness. Human rights function precisely to protect and enhance human beings as bearers of human dignity *qua* the capacity for friendliness (Metz 2011). Thaddeus Metz is the leading proponent of the moral status view of human rights, or what he would probably describe as the friendliness view of human rights.

Second, we have the personhood-based interpretation of human rights (Ikuenobe 2017b). This interpretation of human rights draws from, defends, and advances Menkiti's notion of personhood as the basis to rethink both human dignity and human rights. This approach to African moral-political theory emphasizes responsibilities tethered to acquiring personhood (or virtue) and contributing to communal well-being as the basis for recognizing and actualising human dignity and human rights. In this view, human rights derive and cannot be separated from our responsibilities associated with contributing to the common good, which involves ensuring the well-being of all citizens. The concept of personhood is one that promotes responsibilities, and, in turn, it embodies a duty-centered approach to human dignity and human rights (Ikuenobe 2018). Polycarp Ikuenobe is the leading thinker of the personhood approach to human dignity and human rights among contemporary scholars, where personhood, human dignity and human rights are merited in a community.

Finally, there is the African recognition theory of human rights (Allsobrook 2023). In this view, human rights do not derive from essential facets of human nature. In fact, human nature is the wrong candidate to account for human rights. Human rights are the kinds of things that are negotiated in our lived experience in contingent communities. Human rights emerge and evolve in human cultures as practices to protect human beings from suffering and various threats in their contexts, i.e., our political norms of human rights are a function of normative customary practices that over time have been codified and normalized into law (Allsobrook 2020). It is the recognition of certain customary practices that creates human rights, which serve as conventional means to respect human dignity. In this view, human

[2] I urge the reader to mind the distinction between the moral status and status approach to human rights. The former locates human rights in some value intrinsic to a human being and the latter basis it on the position/rank one occupies in a social order (Rosen 2012; Waldron 2013).

rights are inventions of communities as they search for the common good associated with human welfare.

In total, the book will provide a picture of human rights in African philosophy by considering five political theories of them.[3] All these theories of human rights, in one way or another, share the feature of basing it on the concept of a person salient in African philosophy. It is crucial however to notice that the first four theories, in a sense, may be said to be naturalist in that they consider a feature of human nature to be essential to the ground human rights (Griffin 2008). All these theories of human rights, in one way or another, share the feature of basing it on the concept of a person salient in African philosophy. It is crucial, however, to notice that the first four theories, in a sense, may be said to be naturalist in that they consider a feature of human nature to be essential to ground human rights (Griffin 2008). The four theories differ in terms of what constitutes a plausible account of a person; they also advance different theories of human rights. The last theory provides a non-naturalist interpretation of Menkiti's conception of a person to ground human dignity and human rights. Human dignity as a criterion for human rights is grounded in our shared experience as human beings, not an attribute of an individual. It believes that African cultures, like any other culture, have customary practices that gesture towards recognizing human rights oriented towards realizing the common good.

The debate concerning the correct ontology to ground rights, naturalism or non-naturalism, is still an open one in African philosophy. Scholars of African thought still have to engage in the debate of whether physical or non-physical property secures the best account for human rights. It is worth noting, however, that most scholars (four of the theories of human rights considered in this book) prefer naturalists accounts of human rights over non-naturalist ones (this book will only consider one non-naturalist account) because scholars tend to lean on the former rather than the latter. This provides a ripe opportunity for scholars of African thought to intervene in this under-explored aspect of the debate.

Next, I turn to methodological issues.

[3] I inform the reader that there is another salient interpretation of human rights that does not feature in this book—the vitalist interpretation of human rights (see Metz 2012; Molefe 2022). The major reason why I excluded it in the book is that all the theories considered here are naturalist in their orientation, and, in my view, the vitalist view of human rights is supernaturalist in its orientation. I am aware of attempts to provide a naturalist interpretation of the vitalist view of human rights, I have not found them to be interesting and worthwhile. Readers that may want to explore the vitalist view may consider the following literature (Magesa 1997; Bujo 2001; Metz 2012; Molefe 2017; Lougheed 2025).

Methodological Issues

There are two central methodological issues worth clarifying in this book. The first issue pertains to the use of the term Africa. Second, I will clarify the methodology I will be using to engage in the exposition of the conversations and debates on human rights in African philosophy.

Comments on the Use of 'Africa'

There is a tendency to describe certain ideas or practices using the moniker Africa in literature and ordinary life. In ordinary life, we might refer to some food or restaurant as African. In the intellectual landscape, for example, we refer to *African* philosophy, *Africa*n ethics, or even *African* thought. The term Africa has the potential to invite confusion when its use is not clarified, contextualized and justified. To avoid confusion and justify the proper use of the term Africa, I will rely on Mogobe Ramose's philosophical cogitations on the term. I find his philosophical elucidations on the term Africa useful as a guide, and it informs how I will use it in the book. In the essay 'I doubt, therefore African philosophy exists,' Ramose (2003) makes a case for why we ought to continue using the term Africa in the context of African philosophy despite its negative history.

He begins by informing us that the origins of the use of the term African can be traced to the Greeks and Romans. If this claim is true, it makes it clear that the term Africa is not African, in the sense that indigenous people from the continent did not coin it. It is Europeans, cultural outsiders, that came up with the name Africa. Ramose further informs us that when they used this term, the primary reference or meaning of its use tended to focus on the weather conditions of the place. Ramose contests the use of the term Africa which limits its use to exclusively focus on the weather conditions to the exclusion of its peoples, histories, and cultures. A weather-centered use of the term, according to Ramose, both slights the dignity of the people of this place and erases them as subjects and objects of histories and narratives. The slight of their dignity is a function of minding the weather as if it is more important than the very real and present human beings—to use the name African to focus on weather is fundamentally dehumanizing.

Despite the non-African origins of the term Africa and the dehumanizing use of the term Africa, Ramose and other people in this place, have insisted that we have good grounds to continue to use it. Ramose urges us as the people of the continent to continue using the name Africa. Nevertheless, when we do so, we should be mindful of the moral and political responsibilities associated with maintaining its use. Continuing to use the name has both negative and positive practical implications. The negative practical implications involve the repudiation of all arbitrary and external impositions that aim to denigrate our humanity, our cultures, and our home, Africa. We should not wrongly interpret the rejection of both internal and external impositions to involve even the rejection of the positive contributions from other peoples and cultures outside of Africa. Surely, Africans have a lot to learn from other peoples, cultures and civilizations. We, therefore, should espouse positive elements from other cultures and even exchanges and borrowings based on the values of democracy, transparency, equality, and dialogue are welcome and necessary for human development (Gyekye 1995).

The positive practical implications of continuing with the use of the Africa. Ramose points us to the chief responsibility that revolves around the crucial value of self-determination. The destiny of African people has largely been influenced by external forces. The call now is for Africans to be responsible for their own identity, mission and destiny in the world. No more should Africans be beggars waiting for crumbs to fall from those sitting in the table of nations determining their own affairs and of the future of the world. Africans must determine their own agenda regarding their own issues and future. Moreover, they must also have a voice to contribute to global affairs.

As much as the project of retaining the name Africa has negative and positive practical components, we must try by all means to circumvent potential abuses associated with its adoption and use. We may continue to use the term Africa, but must shun by all means necessary the tendency to romanticize and essentialize it (Matolino 2014). Taking the name Africa seriously involves not working with the romantic picture of our history, culture, and political situations. The example of romanticizing Africa occurs often when we reflect on its pre-colonial period. The tendency is to relate to this period as a blazing history of human, political, and economic perfection. Moreover, a backwards-looking moral and political view suggests that the solutions for a better future for this place are entirely in reclaiming some of its historical legacies and wisdom (Ramose 2009). Bernard Matolino and Wenclaus Kwindingwi (2013) refer to this backwards-looking political approach as a *narrative of return*, and they argue that such attempts have failed dismally to provide a sound socio-economic and political policy for the continent.

Another tendency we must avoid and repudiate involves attempts to misrepresent the place of Africa. This over-simplification occurs when we regard the peoples and cultures of this vast place as homogenous, bearing no diversities and complexities characteristic of all human cultures. The unfortunate moral consequence of such simplifications amounts to dehumanising and degrading the dignity of the people and their cultures. Africans are as human as any other human beings and do have the capacities and dispositions to do all that all other human beings can do. African history bears testimony to moments of wars, peace, stability, industry and trade, rich cultural practices in their diversity and many other crucial elements associated with human existence.

Beyond avoiding negative tendencies concerning the use of the term Africa, a more creative approach to using the term Africa involves associating its people, among others, with thought, where we relate to Africa in terms of the intersection of thought and place. To relate to Africa in terms of the intersection between thought and place represents the espousal of humanity that can self-determine and chart a new path and destiny beyond the history of colonisation. Suppose plurality, complexity, and dynamicity, among others, become our point of departure in providing content to the term Africa. In that case, it should be expected that the term Africa will always have a contested dimension as we debate it from our different vantage points concerning the meanings we can associate with it. What Ramose (2002) describes as 'a *struggle* for reason', which involves the task to self-define-and-determine should be understood as a struggle precisely because it (the term Africa) perennially has the contested element as an essential part of it.

In addition to Ramose's insights on why and how to use the term Africa properly, I also consider common and plausible uses of it by other scholars of African thought (Oyowe 2014; Ikuenobe 2016). Oritsegbubemi Oyowe (2014: 333) explains the two meanings associated with the term Africa in this fashion, "One picks out a geographical category merely while the other refers to a family of ideas distinctive of cultures in the geographical area denoted as Africa.". The term Africa, at least according to Oyowe, has two distinct denotations. The first denotation refers to a place, location, or geography occupied by a people with its own experiences, histories, and cultures (Janz 2009). A place is concrete and located somewhere on the map. The second meaning of Africa refers to 'a family of ideas distinctive of cultures' in a place. The second meaning suggests that places have both elements of diversity within them and those of commonalities, and Oyowe refers to commonalities as a 'family of ideas distinctive' to Africa.

Scholars of African thought tend to associate it with a family of ideas that are distinctive and representative of its intellectual and axiological orientation (Wiredu 1980; Metz 2007). These societies tend to be characterized by the following values: they think of society using family analogies, they tend to prize greetings as a form of respect and social recognition, they are typically characterized by moral partialism, where special relationships like family take priority in a moral context, in the context of punishment they are inclined to reformatory rather than punitive measures. In terms of governance, they favour decision-making on the basis of consensus over majoritarianism, among others (Gyekye 1992; Wiredu 1992).

The claim is that some of these values are prominent in the sub-Saharan African context. They are prominence does not suggest that occurs everywhere in Africa nor that it is exclusive to it. Instead, it indicates the prevalence of this idea in Africa more than in other places (Metz 2007). In this chapter and book, I will be using the idea of Africa to capture both elements, to refer, on the one hand, to a location or place on the map and, on the other, to a family of intuitions and ideas that are salient in it informed by the literature and my experience as a cultural insider (Wiredu 1980; Gyekye 1995; Oyowe 2014). For the purpose of this book, I will regard Africa as a place that has experiences, ideas, and theories, a family of ideas, that can contribute to conversations on human rights. Personhood is one example of a salient idea in African intellectual culture that is relevant and has shaped the debates concerning the relation between the individual and community and the very idea of community. This idea will also feature significantly in this book as we engage the idea of human rights.

Analytical Philosophy

Now that I have clarified the use of the term Africa, I proceed to the discussion of the method I will be using to engage in conversations and debates on human rights. This book belongs to the body of work that contributes to what I describe as 'African analytical philosophy'. I employ the phrase 'African analytical philosophy' to refer to scholars in the context of African philosophy who use the analytic method of doing philosophy (Owolabi 1999). There is a growing body of work that tends to use the techniques of analytic philosophy in the context of African philosophy (Wiredu 1980, 1996; Gyekye 1995, 1997; Matolino 2014, 2019; Molefe 2019, 2021; Oyowe 2021; Metz 2022; Attoe 2022). The techniques of analytical philosophy are typically characterized by two features, namely, linguistic or conceptual analysis and argumentation (Molefe 2015). Language, specifically concepts, serves as a tool through which we make sense of the world. Concepts allow us to search and construct meaning and truth. Concepts allow us to describe and attach values to things in the world. Linguistic or conceptual analysis involves breaking down concepts into their elements in order to understand, define, and use them correctly in the quest for clarity in meaning and in the quest to approximate the truth.

If we do not use language correctly, we may never be able to properly grasp the issues, problems, and puzzles, which may serve as an obstacle in our search for meaning and truth. The assertion by Gyekye (1992: 242–243) is illuminating concerning what conceptual analysis involves—

> Philosophy is a conceptual response to the problems posed in any given epoch for a given society. It is therefore appropriate, even imperative, for contemporary African philosophers to grapple at the conceptual level with the problems and issues of their times, not least of which are the problems of government and political stability.

Gyekye construes philosophy as a conceptual response, whose major service involves dispelling confusions and unclarities in relation to issues occasioned by human experiences. If the concept of personhood, for example, is crucial in the conversations on human rights, then it will be crucial that we analyze it with the intention to contribute meaningfully to our philosophical task to give a picture of human rights in African philosophy. We will need to identify important concepts, define them, and clarify how they are engaged and debated in the literature to gain access to clarity and truth, or at least approximate this intellectual goal.

Philosophy often involves more than just the clarity of ideas and issues; it also provides reasons or evidence to support or justify one's claims/views—this refers to the aspect of argument. An argument essentially involves justifying one's claims or providing reasons for why we should take a certain view seriously. A view, claim, or theory is plausible to the extent that it has rational credibility, i.e., sufficient reasons to support it. The stronger the reasons in favour of a claim, the more we have a basis to accept it as plausible. However, if the reasons justifying a particular claim are less than sufficient, we have a good basis to reject it. Reasons are the currency that philosophers accept as the standard of acceptability or plausibility of claims. Metz

(2007: 378) exemplifies how plausibility (via a quality of reason) works in the analytic tradition:

> … the method of positing of a general principle, posing a particular counterexample, reformulating the general principle so as to avoid the counterexample, posing a new counterexample to the reformulated principle, revising the principle yet again, and so on. That is the kind of methodology I have in mind when I speak of seeking to achieve my aim in a 'systematic, analytic way'…

The aim of the argumentative aspect involves testing a claim against counter claims. The more a claim can address the concerns of the counter claim, the more plausible we may consider it to be, and the opposite is also true.

Now that we have noted that the techniques of analytic philosophy are characterised by conceptual analysis and argumentation, I make one final submission concerning this book. The book aims to give the reader a picture of the status of the conversations and debates on human rights in African philosophy. The aim does not include arguing for a particular picture as the most plausible. Hence, the book will emphasise conceptual analysis over argumentation. We may understand this book to be engaged in the philosophical exposition of assumptions, ideas and arguments on human rights in African philosophy, which will involve systematically clarifying salient views on human rights in this tradition of philosophy. As noted above, we will explore five theories of human rights in African philosophy. Though the book does not emphasise the argumentative element in its approach to human rights, it will attempt to give a lucid and coherent representation of the salient theories of human rights in African philosophy.

Below, I consider the structure of the book.

Structure of the Book

The book is divided into four chapters. I will divide theories on human rights in terms of those that are classical and contemporary in African philosophy. The second chapter will concentrate on classical theories. The focus here will be on the Menkiti-Gyekye debate in African philosophy. This is the debate that has shaped much of the discourse in African philosophy, particularly the debate on the concepts of personhood, human dignity and human rights. Ifeanyi Menkiti is associated with radical communitarianism, which tends to prize the common good as primary and considers human rights to be secondary. Kwame Gyekye's moderate communitarianism considers human rights and duties to enjoy equal moral status in African political thought. The third chapter discusses the contemporary interpretations of human rights in African philosophy. It will consider the contribution of Thaddeus Metz (2011), who proposes the friendliness approach to human rights. It will also consider Polycarp Ikuenobe's (2018) personhood-based account of human rights. Finally, the chapter considers Christopher Allsobrook's (2023) recognition theory of human rights. In the final analysis, I hope the reader will get a picture of human rights in African philosophy. Though the book is not evaluative and argumentative in its form, it will consider prima facie strengths and weaknesses of the various theories in African political thought. The concluding chapter will highlight major themes and debates that can take the conversation forward concerning human rights in African philosophy.

References

Ake, C. 1987. The African Context of Human Rights. *Africa Today* 34:5–12.

Allsobrook, C. 2020. Consensual Recognition of Universal Rights in African Custom. In *The African Other Philosophy, Justice and the Self*, ed. A. Olivier, 21–32. New York: Routledge.

Allsobrook, C. 2023. African Recognition of Dignity as a basis for Universal Human Rights. *Acta Academica* 55:20–40.

Attoe, D. A. 2022. *Towards a New Kind of African Metaphysics: The Idea of Pre-Deterministic Historicity*. Cham: Palgrave Macmillan.

Beitz, C. 2009. *The Idea of Human Rights*. Oxford: Oxford University Press.

Biko, S. 2004. *I Write What I Like: A Selection of his Writings*. Johannesburg: Picador Africa. (Original work published 1978).

Bujo, B. 2001. *Foundations of an African Ethic*. Translated by B. McNeil. New York: Crossroad Publishers.

Chemhuru, M. 2018. African Communitarianism and Human Rights: Towards a Compatibilist View. *Theoria* 65:37–56.

Chimakonam, J. O. 2017. African Philosophy and Global Epistemic Injustice. *Journal of Global Ethics* 13 (2): 120–137.

Cobbah, J. A. 1987. African Values and the Human Rights Debate: An African Perspective. *Human Rights Quarterly* 9 (3): 309–331.

Deng, F. 2004. Human Rights in the African Context. In *Companion to African Philosophy*, ed. K. Wiredu, 499–508. Oxford: Blackwell.

Donnelly, J. 1982. Human Rights as Natural Rights. *Human Rights Quarterly* 4 (3): 391–405.

Donnely, J. 2009. *Human Dignity and Human Rights*. Denver: Josef Korbel School of International Studies.

Feinberg, J. 1971. The Nature and Value of Rights. *The Journal of Value Inquiry* 4:243–457.

Freeman, M. 2022. *Human Rights*. Wiley.

Fricker, M. 2007. *Epistemic Injustice: Power and the Ethics of Knowing*. Oxford University Press.

Graness, A. 2015. Is the Debate on 'Global Justice' a Global One? Some Considerations in View of Modern Philosophy in Africa. *Journal of Global Ethics* 11 (1): 126–140.

Griffin, J. 2008. *On Human Rights*. Oxford: Oxford University Press.

Gyekye, K. 1992. Person and Community in African Thought. In *Person and Community: Ghanaian Philosophical Studies*, ed. K. Wiredu and Gyekye, 101–122. Washington, DC: Council for Research in Values and Philosophy.

Gyekye, K. 1995. *An Essay on African Philosophical Thought: The Akan Conceptual Scheme*. Philadelphia: Temple University Press.

Gyekye, K. 1997. *Tradition and Modernity: Philosophical Reflections on the African Experience*. New York: Oxford University Press.

Habermas, J. 2010. The Concept of Human Dignity and the Realistic Utopia of Human Rights. *Metaphilosophy*. 4:464–480.

Hopgood, S., J. Snyder, and L. Vinjamuri. 2017. *Human Rights Futures*. Cambridge University Press.

Hughes, G. 2011. The Concept of Dignity in the Universal Declaration of Human Rights. *Journal of Religious Ethics* 39:1–24.

Ikuenobe, P. 2016. The Communal Basis for Moral Dignity: An African Perspective. *Philosophical Papers* 45:437–469.

Ikuenobe, P. 2017a. Matolino's Misunderstanding of Menkiti's African Moral View of the Person and Community. *South African Journal of Philosophy* 36:553–567.

Ikuenobe, P. 2017b. The Communal Basis for Moral Dignity: An African Perspective. *Philosophical Papers* 45:437–469.

Ikuenobe, P. 2018. Human Rights, Personhood, Dignity, and African Communalism. *Journal of Human Rights* 17 (5): 589–604.

Ilesanmi, O. 2001. Human Rights Discourse in Modern Africa: A Comparative Religious Perspective. *Journal of Religious Ethics* 23:293–320.

Janz, B. B. 2009. *Philosophy in An African Place*. Rowman & Littlefield.

Kaphagawani, D. 2004. African Conceptions of a Person: A Critical Survey. In *Companion to African Philosophy*, ed. K. Wiredu, 332–442. Oxford: Blackwell Publishing.

Lougheed, K. 2025. African Vital Force and the Permissibility of Euthanasia. *Journal of Medical Ethics* 51(4):233–238.

Magesa, L. 1997. *African Religion: The Moral Traditions of Abundant Life*. New York: Orbis Books.

Masolo, D. 2010. *Self and Community in a Changing World*. Indianapolis: Indiana University Press.

Matolino, B. 2014. *Personhood in African Philosophy*. Pietermaritzburg: Cluster Publications.

Matolino, B. 2019. *Afro-Communitarian Democracy*. Bloomsbury Publishing PLC.

Matolino, B., and W. Kwindingwi. 2013. The End of Ubuntu. *South African Journal of Philosophy* 32:197–120.

Menkiti, I. 1984. Person and Community in African Traditional Thought. In *African Philosophy:An Introduction*, ed. R. A. Wright, 171–118. Lanham: University Press of America.

Menkiti, I. A. 2004. On the Normative Conception of a Person. *A Companion to African Philosophy* 324–331.

Menkiti, I. 2017. Community, Communism, Communitarianism: An African Intervention. *The Palgrave Handbook of African Philosophy* 461–473.

Metz, T. 2007. Toward an African Moral Theory. *Journal of Political Philosophy* 15 (3): 321–341.

Metz, T. 2011. Ubuntu as a Moral Theory and Human Rights in South Africa. *African Human Rights Law Journal* 11:532–559.

Metz, T. 2012. An African Theory of Moral Status: A Relational Alternative to Individualism and Holism. *Ethical Theory Moral Practice: International Forum* 14:387–400.

Metz, T. 2022. *A Relational Moral Theory: African Ethics in and Beyond the Continent*. Oxford: Oxford University Press.

Molefe, M. 2015. *Explorations in African Meta-Ethics: Can a Case Be Made for a Supernaturalist Position?* [Doctoral dissertation]. University of Johannesburg, Johannesburg.

Molefe, M. 2017. Relational ethics and partiality: A critique of Thad Metz's "Towards an African Moral theory." *Theoria: A Journal of Social and Political Theory* 64(152):53–76.

Molefe, M. 2018. Personhood and Rights in an African Tradition. *Politikon* 45(2):217–231.

Molefe, M. 2019. *An African Philosophy of Personhood, Morality and Politics*. New York: Palgrave Macmillan.

Molefe, M. 2021. African Ethics and Agent-Centred Duties. In *Essays on Contemporary Issues in African Philosophy* (pp. 107–124). Cham: Springer International Publishing.

Molefe, M. 2022. *Human Dignity in African Philosophy, A Very Short Introduction*. New York: Springer.

Mudimbe, V. Y. 1988. *The Invention of Africa: Gnosis, Philosophy, and the Order of Knowledge*. Bloomington: Indiana University Press.

Naim, Abd Allah Ahmad, and F. Deng. 1990. *Human Rights in Africa: Cross-Cultural Perspectives*. Brookings Institution.

Owolabi, K. 1999. Orientations in African Philosophy: A Critical Survey. *Indian Philosophical Quarterly* 26(1).

Oyowe, A. 2014. An African Conception of Human Rights? Comments on the Challenges of Relativism. *Human Rights Review* 15:329–347.

Oyowe, O. A. 2021. Social Persons and the Normativity of Needs. In *Towards an African Political Philosophy of Needs*, ed. M. Molefe and C. Allsobrook. Cham: Palgrave Macmillan.
Ramose, M. B. 2002. The Struggle for Reason in Africa. In *Philosophy from Africa: A Text with Readings*, ed. P. H. Coetzee and A. P. J. Roux, 1–18, 2nd edn. Southern Africa: Oxford University Press.
Ramose, M. B. 2003. The Philosophy of Ubuntu and Ubuntu as Philosophy. In *Philosophy from Africa: A Text with Readings*, ed. P. H. Coetzee and A. P. J. Roux, 230–237, 2nd edn. Oxford University Press Southern Africa.
Ramose, M. B. 2009. Globalization and Ubuntu. *Epistemologies of the South* 2:175–220.
Rosen, M. 2012. *Dignity: Its History and Meaning*. Cambridge, MA: Harvard University Press.
Toscano, M. 2011. Human Dignity as High Moral Status. *Les ateliers de l'éthique* 6 (2): 4–25.
Waldron J. 1987. Can Communal Goods be Human Rights? *European Journal of Sociology* 28(2):296–322.
Waldron, J. 2013. *Is Dignity the Foundation of Human Rights?* New York University Public Law and Legal Theory Working Papers. Paper 374. Accessed 18 November 2022.
Wiredu, K. 1980. *Philosophy and an African Culture*. Cambridge: Cambridge University Press.
Wiredu, K. 1992. Moral Foundations of an African Culture. In *Person and Community: Ghanaian Philosophical Studies*, ed. K. Wiredu and K. Gyekye, 193–206. Washington, DC: The Council for Research in Values and Philosophy.
Wiredu, K. 1996. *Cultural Universals and Particulars: An African Perspective*. Indianapolis: Indiana University Press.

Chapter 2
Classical Theories of Human Rights

Introduction

The chapter explores the conversations and debates on human rights in African philosophy. It specifically focuses on what I describe as the 'classical' theories of human rights in African philosophy. I regard the theories by Ifeanyi Menkiti and Kwame Gyekye as 'classical' since they were among the first written contributions in the English-speaking literature on human rights in African philosophy (Matolino 2014). The literature tends to construe Ifeanyi Menkiti's philosophical contribution to personhood, ethics and Afro-communitarianism to amount to the political view of radical communitarianism (Gyekye 1992; Oyowe 2014). Menkiti could be construed to be advocating for a duty-based political theory that assigns a secondary status to human rights. Gyekye, on the other hand, articulates a dual conception of personhood (i.e., it is composed of individual and relational features), and he accounts for the relation between the individual and community that amounts to the political theory of moderate communitarianism (Gyekye 1997). In this view, duties and rights have equal status (although when the two clash the former ought to take priority). This chapter will focus on the debate between radical and moderate communitarianism to provide the reader with a picture of human rights in African philosophy.

The debates associated with classical theories of human rights, radical and moderate communitarianism, are concerned at least with two related questions. First, in very general terms, the debate pivots on drawing from indigenous cultural, epistemic, and axiological resources to construct a plausible philosophical account of Afro-communitarianism. Post-colonial leaders and intellectuals in Africa have been at pains to construct a plausible vision of a good or just social arrangement to reverse the socio-political and economic ruins caused by the colonial invasion (Gyekye 1992; Wiredu 2009). The conversation about Afro-communitarianism, captured in the debate between radical and moderate communitarianism, should be understood

M. Molefe, *An Introduction to Human Rights in African Philosophy*, SpringerBriefs in Ethics, https://doi.org/10.1007/978-3-032-04447-1_2

as a post-colonial search for a vision of a good society in African political thought (Wiredu 2009). The indigenous and axiological term that is pivotal in the debate between radical and moderate communitarianism is that of personhood (or, African personhood).

Second, the debates on Afro-communitarianism specifically investigate the question of whether human rights ought to have a place in a plausible conception of Afro-communitarian political theory. Hence, the chapter will provide a systematic exposition of radical and moderate communitarianism as philosophical attempts to include and justify human rights in Afro-communitarianism. One of the things we will observe is that different conceptions of personhood have varying consequences for our conception of human rights.

I stipulate that a meaningful exposition of human rights in African philosophy must cover the following essential components of the debates on human rights. First, it must consider the status and relevance of human rights in Afro-communitarianism. Typically, communitarian societies and theories from both the African and Eastern cultures tend to repudiate human rights as proper political instruments to imagine and manage political communities (Donnelly 1982; Ake 1987). Note, for example, Alisdare MacIntyre (1982) considers rights to be fiction much like a unicorn is a creation of our imagination but does not exist in reality. It will be interesting to paint a picture of human rights to consider whether Afro-communitarianism considers them to be real, legitimate and necessary political instruments to imagine and manage political communities. Two observations will unfold regarding the status of rights in Afro-communitarian thought: (a) generally, scholars that espouse Afro-communitarianism endorse human rights as significant political tools to imagine a just society and (b) the significance they associate with human rights tend to differ in the one dominant in the Euro-American political tradition.

Second, the literature in political philosophy on human rights tends to be divided along the lines of naturalism or non-naturalism (Freeman 1995). Naturalism grounds human rights on some facets of human nature such as rationality, capabilities, image of god, and so on (Donnelly 1982; Griffin 2008). Non-naturalism considers human rights to be a construction of culture or society (Freeman 1995). This chapter will help us to understand the position of classical theories in the divide between naturalism and non-naturalism regarding human rights. The chapter will indicate that classical theories tend to espouse a naturalist interpretation of human rights in African philosophy. Third, concerning the naturalist interpretation, we must specify the relevant natural property or endowments that account for human rights. Finally, the literature in philosophy tends to stipulate a relationship between human dignity and human rights (Donnelly 2009; Hughes 2011). This chapter will also explore whether such a relationship is anticipated in African political thought. The chapter will indicate that such a relationship is existent in African political thought albeit remains theoretically underdeveloped.

It is important to insert a disclaimer about the aims of this chapter and the book in general. The aim of this chapter is not to give the most plausible account of human rights in African philosophy. The aim is not to defend some vision or version of human rights in light of African thought. The aim, rather, is a moderate one, which involves providing a picture or an introduction to the theme of human rights in African philosophy. In this chapter, the picture will be limited to the conversations and debates as they involve radical and moderate communitarianism. The first section will elucidate on radical communitarianism. The second section will expound on moderate communitarianism. The final section will reflect on the Menkiti-Gyekye debate, considering the reflections of leading scholars in African political thought, such as Bernard Matolino, Polycarp Ikuenobe, Motsamai Molefe, and Oritsegbubemi Oyowe. This reflection aims to ascertain the status and place of human rights in African philosophy.

Radical Communitarianism

We must begin by categorically stating that Menkiti has never defined his political view on human rights in terms of 'radical communitarianism'. Gyekye (1992: 103), in his analysis of Menkiti's adumbrations on personhood and political thought, argued that it should be described as "radical/extreme communitarianism". He arrived at this conclusion because he believed that Menkiti offered an incorrect conception of personhood in African philosophy. His major gripe is that Menkiti's interpretation of personhood, and its implications for moral-political theory, tends to exaggerate the importance of the community concerning the relation between the individual and community. The fact that Menkiti assigns a secondary status to human rights in African political thought also justifies describing his view (and of some post-colonial leaders) as a radical or extreme version of communitarianism, at least according to Gyekye.

To contextualize and appreciate the description of Menkiti's political view in terms of radical communitarianism, we can follow four themes that stand out in the essay that earned his work on personhood, ethics and political theory the label of radical communitarianism. First, his conception of a person. Second, his understanding of the relationship between the individual and community. Third, his understanding of the social and political community. Finally, the place of human rights in a political communitarian scheme.

Menkiti on Personhood

In the essay 'Person and community in African traditional thought,' which is typically criticized by scholars for embodying radical communitarianism, Menkiti (1984) aims to articulate an African concept of a person. It is not immediately clear whether Menkiti was just after one concept of a person in African thought or several of them; at least this is my view (Molefe 2019, 2020, 2021). In my reading of the essay under consideration, I identify at least four distinct senses of a person (and I must hasten to add that Menkiti does not always clarify or appear to be aware of them). Immediately, I identify the ordinary day-to-day use of the term person. In this sense, it refers to human beings, a thing like you and me, the reader of this book. I doubt that there can ever be any meaningful engagement on the concept of a person in African thought that does not take this idea of a person as a human being as a point of departure (i.e., it seems to be presupposed in all discussion on personhood, particularly in the context of human rights).

One does not need to be a rocket scientist to be aware of this notion of a person as a human being. In fact, in several places, Menkiti (1984: 171) indicates that he is aware of it by distinguishing a biological organism and the status of a person. The former is merely biological, a thing born of human parentage with particular biological and ontological features characteristic of humankind, a human being. The latter notion refers to a thing that emerges after a process of socio-moral transformation, a moral agent whose conduct and character is virtuous (Menkiti 2004). In other words, though these two concepts of a person are distinct, they are intrinsically related; it is the development of the former that amounts to the emergence of the latter (Bewaji and Ramose 2003; Oyowe 2022).

The above-mentioned distinction also covers the second notion of a person—the normative concept of a person. In the first sense, personhood makes reference to a specific biological or ontological kind, the human species, things like me and you, the reader of this book. In the second sense, personhood refers to a moral agent that has successfully engaged in the process of socio-moral development to acquire virtue. Menkiti associates this notion of personhood with excellence, specifically having a virtuous disposition (Behrens 2013; Oyowe 2013). In fact, he uses the word excellence four times to explain the kind of moral development associated with personhood (1984: 172 & 173). Personhood is something the moral agent acquires or nurtures in the form of good character or a virtuous disposition (Ikuenobe 2006). Depending on the quality of one's conduct, the agent could either gain or lose personhood. Menkiti (1984: 172) refers to this concept of a person as a "maximalist" conception of a person, which denotes that biological and ontological features, in and of themselves, are not sufficient to capture this sense of personhood. Maximalist conception requires the development of our biological and ontological features. The literature refers to this idea of a person as the normative concept of a person (Wiredu 1996; Kapaghawani 2004; Ikuenobe 2006; Matolino 2014; Molefe 2019). It is the normative notion of a person that seems to be central in Menkiti's exposition of personhood in African philosophy. It is important to observe that there are two other concepts of a person in his exposition.

Another ontological notion of a person is the idea of a personal identity. Personal identity concerns the question of what makes the agent the same person (individual) over time (Metz 2013). If one is interacting with me at different times, it is reasonable that they may assume that they are dealing with the same person across these different moments of engagement (particularly, if we have met frequently and have exchanged crucial identifying information about each other). In subsequent engagement, there is no need, or at least we behave so, to establish if we are dealing with the same person. The kind of personhood anticipated is the one that is lost when someone loses their memory or certain cognitive abilities—this is perfectly demonstrated in the famous Phineas Cage case. One can meaningfully say 's/he is no longer her/himself' referring to a loss of personal identity. What is lost is their personhood *qua* personal identity. I think Menkiti (1984: 172) has this idea of personhood in mind when he opines,

> ... the individual comes to see himself as man, and it is by first knowing this community as a stubborn perduring fact of the psychophysical world that the individual also comes to know himself as a durable, more or less permanent, fact of this world.

The claim here points us to the process of socialization, and culturalization, which amounts to the human agent gaining self-awareness in the context of a cultural community. The pre-existence of the community provides a basis for self- and social awareness—I am because we are. He proceeds to associate the emergence of self-awareness with other important features of personal identity in this fashion, "also the language which he speaks, and which is no small factor in the constitution of his mental dispositions and attitudes, belong to this or that specific human group" (ibid.). This self-awareness is connected with language, which also indicates and is expressive of belonging to a particular cultural group, be it Zulus, or Sothos. Finally, Menkiti rubber-stamps this interpretation of a person to involve personal identity, when he avers, "What is more, the sense of *self-identity* which the individual comes to possess cannot be made sense of except by reference to these collective facts" (ibid., emphasis mine). Here, Menkiti discusses the concept of a person as a personal identity. In fact, he propounds a communitarian conception of personal identity, where it is a function (entirely) of certain collective or communal facts that socializes and humanizes the human agent. That is, personal identity is a function entirely of being enmeshed in robust social relationships (Wiredu 1996).

There is another distinct sense of a person in Menkiti's essay that we might describe as a capacity-based concept of a person. Often, in this concept of a person, the mere possession of the relevant capacity is value-endowing (Muade 2023). Scholars typically use the technical term of moral status to refer to the capacity-based value endowing notion of a person (Behrens 2013; Molefe 2019). The capacity-based notion of a person is evident in Menkiti's engagement with John Rawls' conception of social justice. In John Rawls' view, at least as interpreted by Menkiti, only persons can participate in social justice. Menkiti (1984: 178, emphasis mine) cites Rawls approvingly in this fashion,

> [E]qual justice is owed to those who have the *capacity* to take part in and to act in accordance with the public understanding of the initial situation . . . The sufficient condition for equal justice [is] the *capacity* for moral personality.

Among other things, justice is a reserve for those who have the capacity or potential to enter into a social contract. It is not the actual entering into the initial situation that secures one a place in a social contract; rather, it is a moral personality that one has merely because she possesses the relevant ontological endowments or capacities. In Rawls' view, the relevant ontological capacity is reason or rationality (Kittay 2005). Rationality is the pre-condition for participating in social justice. Those individuals who have the capacity for reason, or what he describes as moral personality, are owed respect as persons. The notion of a person under consideration is ethical in nature in that those who have this capacity are owed moral respect, which both Rawls and Menkiti tethered to social justice. This capacity-based concept of a person is dominant in the Euro-American literature on bioethics, animal ethics, human dignity and human rights, where some object has intrinsic value merely because it possesses relevant ontological capacities (Warren 1997; Metz 2012; Behrens 2013).

We noted four distinct notions of a person in Menkiti's essay on personhood, namely, a person as (a) a human being, (b) virtue, (c) personal identity, and (d) moral status. The common view in the literature is that Menkiti in this essay was aiming to provide an account of the normative conception of a person (see Wiredu 1992, Gyekye 1992; Ikuenobe 2018). Though I am sympathetic to this view, it does not quite explain why Menkiti invokes and makes reference to the other concepts of a person, personal identity, and moral status. At the background of our exploration of Menkiti's political theory and debates on human rights, we should be asking ourselves what notion of a person, among the ones mentioned above, justifies accusing him of espousing radical communitarianism. I will suggest below that it is the notion of personal identity rather than that of moral status that has wrongly been used to sponsor this kind of criticism against his work.

We turn next to consider the relationship between the individual and community in Menkiti's moral philosophy.

Relation Between the Individual and Community

How does Menkiti account for the relationship between the individual and the community? The question typically in African philosophy can be stated in terms of priority i.e., which, between the individual and community, ought to take priority? John Mbiti and Menkiti appear to take the view that the community ought or does take priority over the individual. Note this comment by John Mbiti, "I am because we are, and since we are, therefore I am." (1970: 215). To articulate his conception of a person, Menkiti (2004: 324, emphasis mine) relies on Mbiti's assertion 'I am because we are'. He interprets this assertion in this fashion,

> Its sense is not that of a person speaking on behalf of, or in reference to, another, but rather of an individual, who recognizes the sources of his or her own humanity, and so realizes, with internal assurance, that in the absence of others, no grounds exist for a claim regarding the individual's own standing as a person. The notion at work here is the notion of an extended self.

We are here encountering a relational conception of a person. To be a person or even the very possibility of individuality (biologically and socially) involves being caught up in continuous social relationships with others. The source of the individual's humanity essentially depends on being connected with others. Menkiti (2004: 324) proceeds to affirm the relational view by describing it in terms of "beingness-with-others". Menkiti is very clear that the acquisition of language, human personality, group identity, and many other human abilities, depends precisely on being a part of a human community. It is the human context and interactions therein that make possible the emergence of a human person with all the requisite human functions. Hence, Menkiti (1984: 171) avers, "man is defined by reference to the environing community.".

It would be incorrect to read Menkiti as discounting our inborn human capacities and abilities in a proper account of personal identity and human agency. He appears to recognize these capacities and abilities. For him, they are just the raw material that presents mere potentiality. It is only in the context of human contact in the context of the human community that these can be actualized and their full potential realized in human fellowship. The individual claims to humanity are void without 'because we are.'. With this relational account of a person, we may proceed to consider if it has any implications for how to conceptualize the relationship between the individual and the community. The suggestion that emerges from both Mbiti and Menkiti seems to be that the community entirely defines a person. It is important to ask two questions. What does the claim the community defines or confers personhood mean? How does he understand the idea of a community?

Menkiti's Conception of Community

Remember, for Menkiti, there is no possibility of personhood without the community. He specifies the role of the community as both the catalyst and a prescriber of norms in the process of personhood (1984: 173). Without the community, there is no possibility of personhood. For personhood to emerge, the individual must be caught up with it, in one way or another; other than that, it is impossible. But what is a community? Menkiti distinguishes at least two senses of the term community in light of the Euro-American and African cultures. He explains the Euro-American conception of the community in terms of "constituted human groups" and the African conception in terms of "collectivities in the truest sense" (Menkiti 1984: 179). In the Euro-American conception of a community, there is a sense in which the community is artificial, where individuals come together by force of circumstance or social vicissitudes. In the African context, there is a sense in which the community is a natural or organic part of reality, and it plays a decisive role in the definition and experience of what it means to be a human individual and a person.

To approximate the distinction between these two senses of a community, I will rely on the idea of shared relations (which will also help us to understand what Menkiti and Mbiti probably mean when they say the community defines a person). Specifically, I will distinguish between the Euro-American and African conceptions of a community in terms of how these two intellectual traditions tend to construe shared relations. The idea of shared relations essentially gives us a sense of how to understand two distinct and even competing conceptions of the community. We can draw the distinction between "contingently shared relations" and "essentially shared relations"; the former corresponds with the Euro-American conception of a community and the latter with the African view (Neal & Paris 1990: 425). Contingently shared relations understand persons or selves as essentially separate, apart, and independent from each other. Individual human beings, on this view, are characteristically self-sufficient. The core that defines the person is a function of their individuality (some aspect of their nature, be it rationality or a soul), and it has nothing to do with any other external reference. In this view, shared relations are merely optional (contingent), probably as avenues for the expression or protection of individual human beings, their interests, and their goals.

In this view, relationships are optional avenues for self-expression and protection. The individual does not need the community to be a person. She gets into the community because she is already a person. Her personhood is a settled matter, which is prior to shared relations. Menkiti refers to this conception of a person as an "*additive approach*" of the community, where the individuals with already pre-established interests, goals and ambitions come together, shared relations, to advance their personal interests. This approach to personhood and shared relations is reminiscent of the Hobbesian worldview of the relation between a person and community (or the state). It is a vision of self-interested individuals fearing that on her/his own her/his interests would be at serious risk—the state of nature—s/he conspires with other self-interested individuals to form a political community (the state) that will protect each individual interests. In Menkiti's view, this approach to shared relations does not provide a proper sense of community but a mere "association" of convenience or even efficiency (1984: 180).

Essentially shared relations, on the other hand, are the kinds which are necessary for personhood. Human and personal identity is not possible outside of these shared relationships. The human and personal identity essentially depends on interdependence, interconnectedness and intersubjectivity of selves. To be human just is to be connected with others in a plurality and diversity of relationships, and these relationships come to define the individual. There is no person or personal identity outside and without these relationships. Menkiti (1984: 179) associates an African conception of a community, or shared relations, with Mbiti's expression of it 'I am because we are'. He asserts that the 'we' in this expression encapsulates "*a thoroughly fused collective 'we'*" (ibid.,). Radically, the suggestion is that the component individual cannot make sense of her own human identity, personal identity, projects and goals without essentially referring to shared relations that define her/his world and the possibilities that surround him. Hence, earlier we cited Menkiti commenting on Mbiti's assertion to amount to the claim that the individual's internal assurance of her/his own existence as a self essentially derives and depends on the community—the language, cultural identity, the history, the economy, the rituals, opportunities, and so on, on these shared relations.

In his analysis of Menkiti's conception of the community, Oritsegbubemi Oyowe (2022) describes Menkiti's idea of a community in terms of the idea of a "social architecture". The idea of social architecture refers to a complex layer of relationships characterized by "language, history, social practices, institutions and rules" (Oyowe 2022: 10). The social architecture is an inescapable and defining context of our existence, humanity and personal identity. Without social architecture, or essentially shared relationships, there is no possibility for the emergence of human experiences, meaning and culture. Hence, when Menkiti claims that the community defines a person, he has in mind the complex layer of interconnecting relations that provide the context, scope and cultural resources for humanization and socialization. Without the community, one cannot be a human being. In this sense, the community is an overarching cultural structure that creates possibilities for humanity and human beings.

The Place of Human Rights in Communitarianism

With a picture of Menkiti's conception of a person and the community, we are in a position to unfold the place of human rights in his ethical scheme. According to this reading of Menkiti, personhood is entirely a relational enterprise. It is defined, operationalized, and realized in the social architecture. The normative concept of a person provides us with one way to appreciate the place of human rights in Menkiti's political thought. The normative concept of personhood implies two important ethical concepts that might help us understand Menkiti's political vision. First, we have the concept of duty or responsibility that is intrinsic to the notion of personhood (Wiredu 2009). Second, we have the concept of virtue which is also intrinsic to the normative concept of a person (Gyekye 1992). The two concepts—responsibility/duty and virtue—are connected in the Afro-communitarian ethical scheme. The moral agent has the responsibility or duty to realize their own moral destiny, which is moral perfection, or the acquisition of virtue (Metz 2010).

The responsibility under consideration operates at two levels. On the one hand, it targets the realization of moral development, where the agent nurtures a virtuous disposition. The moral agent has to improve her own character. On the other hand, the responsibility to realize one's truly social nature characterized by relational virtues—generosity, care, love, friendliness—throws one into relationships where s/he can test and develop her character. It is only in robust social relationships that the moral agent can develop her social virtues. The latter consideration brings to the fore the importance of the community in the exercise of responsibilities and the acquisition of virtues. The moral agent engages in the process of transformation necessarily in the context of the community. The community not only proves the social contexts, but Menkiti informs us that it serves as the prescriber of norms and rules of excellence. Moreover, the community provides the resources to empower the agent as s/he engages in the task of personal development. The provision by the community of the rules of engagement (for excellence) and the support to empower moral agents must be appreciated in the context of shared relations. The moral agent must fulfil his duties to the community, and it is the fulfilling of these duties that amounts to the emergence of personhood. Hence, Menkiti (1984: 176) opines, "It is the carrying out of these obligations that transforms one … to the person-status … marked by a widened maturity of ethical sense.".

The carrying out of obligations or duties, as prescribed by the community, leads to the emergence of a virtuous person. So, the idea of personhood, central in Menkiti's moral-political philosophy, imagines the moral agent that connects with others through other-regarding obligations. These other-regarding obligations are meant to contribute to and enhance the social architecture and promote social welfare. Given the duty-oriented ethical notion of a person in the context where one is enmeshed in shared relations, Menkiti (1984: 180) informs us that "African societies tend to be organized around the requirements of duty" to promote and enhance the community. He further states that in this moral-political system duties to the collective take priority over individual rights, and rights take a secondary consideration. The logic of Menkiti's view should be apparent by now. The goal of each moral agent is to acquire personhood. Personhood can be gained only in the community via the exercise of other-regarding duties to enhance the community. The focus and orientation of duties associated with personhood are those expressive of the debt we owe towards others, rather than what others owe us (Molefe 2017).

This overwhelmingly duty-based ethical system does have a place for human rights, but it seems to be a limited one. The claim that rights are secondary should not be wrongly interpreted to suggest that they are not important. They are important, but not a primary moral-political consideration when dealing with matters affecting the common good or the community. Primacy is assigned to duties and obligations towards the community, which essentially involve the benefit and empowerment of all. The implication could be that, all things being equal, moral-political engagements should entirely be addressed by appealing to other-directed duties. However, in situations where the community fails to deliver such goods, human rights can kick in as a remedial measure. Three examples may give us a picture regarding the primacy of duties and the secondary status of human rights.

First, consider the case of a young fellow who gets into a bus, finds a seat, and sits down. A moment later, the bus is full, and there is an old lady who has no seat, and is standing beside him. A duty-based ethical theory associated with personhood would urge the young man to give up his seat, which he has by right since he bought the ticket and arrived first on the bus. The conscience of a duty-based ethics-orientated person, who is orientated towards acquiring virtue, would easily give up his rights to promote the welfare of the older person. The duty to express care and compassion takes precedence over the entitlement to sit on the bus. It would be a serious moral failure on the part of the young fellow to insist on his rights in a context where sympathy and care would benefit the elderly person.

Second, consider a case where some individual owns a piece of property, and they have built a house on it. The state is faced with a housing shortage for the poor, and it requires a propitious land where it can build houses to accommodate its needs. It turns out the piece of land is good for building a small community to redress the condition of homelessness and poverty for the poor. In the communitarian scheme, at least as imagined by Menkiti, the state may overrule the property rights of the individual for the benefit of the greater community. Individual interests will be placed in the context of the greater good scheme in terms of providing shelter and livelihood for the benefit of the greater community. The state may compensate the individual and may find him an alternative place or even integrate her/him with the new community (depending on what is not worse off in terms of the individual's life and livelihood in the context of the community). The idea is not that property rights are not important. Rather, the importance of individuals' property rights cannot hold sway even when they do not further the interests of humanity (or community) but simply focus on the entitlement of the individual. There is a sense that Afro-communitarianism is trying to create a humane world where propitious conditions of existence should be extended to cater to many more people than less, all things being equal. The ideal situation is the creation of social conditions where everyone's basic needs are met, as far as possible.

Finally, consider a case where there is a flagrant violation of human rights. A situation in which the state (or community and citizens) fail to exercise empowering duties towards citizens. In this context, it is justified for individuals to insist on their rights to the state, courts of the land, and even beyond. If the courts of the land are so deteriorated and depraved that they are entirely bent towards injustice and violation of human rights, individuals may protest and protect themselves. The basis of the protest and protection is based on their human rights and their entitlement to freedom and peace. Resistance to apartheid in South Africa is the perfect example of this kind of resistance. Moreover, the individual(s) may justify even requesting the aid of other external parties like the United Nations and other countries for the defence of human rights. In this context, human rights are invoked and insisted upon as a measure of last resort because the community is failing to provide empowering and conducive conditions for human existence.

Moderate Communitarianism and Human Rights

Moderate communitarianism makes two crucial interventions in African philosophy. First, it provides what it considers to be a plausible conception of a person. Second, it argues that a plausible interpretation of Afro-communitarianism ought to have a place for human rights. In Gyekye's exposition of moderate communitarianism, a correct conception of African personhood is a crucial building block for making the case for human rights in African political thought. In fact, Gyekye (1992: 101) informs us that "The type of social structure or arrangement evolved by a particular society seems to reflect—and be influenced by the public conceptions of personhood held in the society." The assertion implies that a correct conception of personhood will probably lead to a correct political arrangement or structure. In Gyekye's view, Menkiti fails to properly appreciate the place of human rights in African political thought because he operates with a defective conception of personhood. Gyekye believes that this is a correct conception of a person, which entails a plausible conception of a political structure that espouses human rights.

In what follows, I do two things. I begin by providing Gyekye's account of personhood. Second, I proceed to demonstrate how his conception of personhood entails a particular conception of human rights.

Gyekye on Personhood

A close reading of Gyekye's contribution to metaphysical, ethical, and political thought in African philosophy indicates several distinct senses of a person. First, the crux of the debate between Gyekye and Menkiti revolves around the relational nature of personhood. Whereas both agree that communitarianism embodies a relational conception of a person, Gyekye argues that a plausible conception ought to accommodate or balance individuality as a feature of a correct conception of a person. He counters the view that personhood is entirely defined by the community. At best, personhood is partly constituted by relationality. He insists that there is a domain of individuality that we must recognize as part of a correct understanding of personhood, and it has a place in a correct conception of Afro-communitarianism. This concept of a person is open to two possible interpretations (or senses), namely, *personal identity* and *moral status*.

According to Gyekye, the correct way to understand personal identity is not only in terms of reference to communal properties. That is, we cannot account for personal identity strictly in terms of external features or cultural resources. Such an account of personhood is less than adequate; it fails to appreciate the crucial ontological equipment that is definitive of the individuality of the person such as the endowments of rationality, volition, and so on (Gyekye 2004). It is the interaction between the communal and individual features that adequately account for personal identity. Concerning moral status, Gyekye argues that some fundamental features of our human nature ground our moral status. That is, individual persons have intrinsic value merely because they possess particular moral qualities or capacities. It is some property of the individual *qua* her natural endowments, such as rationality or autonomy, that secures the moral status of human beings. I will come back to Gyekye's account of moral status.

The third and fourth notions of a person emerge when Gyekye contends against Menkiti's claim that we acquire personhood. Gyekye makes two different claims, and I argue that these claims represent two distinct notions of a person. On the one hand, Gyekye is categorical that we do not acquire personhood. Note this comment, "A human person is a person whatever his age or social status … One is a person because of what he is, not because of what he has acquired." (1992: 108). The sense of a person in this question refers to the fact of being human. Ontologically speaking, one is either a human being or not. We do not acquire the status of a person; it is a function of our nature. We are persons *qua* human status merely because we are born of human parentage. It is crucial to note that we do not earn this kind of personhood; neither can we lose it. In this sense, when we say one is a person, we simply mean they are a particular ontological kind. Specifically, Homo sapiens.

On the other hand, Gyekye is aware of the notion of a person as a property or status that we acquire. Personhood as some kind of acquisition refers to a socio-moral status that we come to possess consequent to the quality of our conduct concerning some standard of excellence. In this sense, one can be denied the status of personhood. When we deny the moral agent the status of personhood, we are judging the individual to have a defective character. When we assert that the moral agent is a person, we are judging them to have a good character. The notion of personhood, in this sense, is an indicator of virtue, or lack thereof. Hence, Gyekye (1992: 110) associates the notion of personhood with "the display of moral virtue" or "the practice of virtue". Each individual is tasked with the socio-moral goal of becoming a person, which involves nurturing their natural endowments to be characterized by virtue. Gyekye (1992: 114) associates personhood with these virtues: "generosity, kindness, compassion, benevolence, respect and concern for others; in fine, any action or behaviour that conduces to the promotion of the welfare of others". Hence, scholars of African thought converge on the view that personhood is something that one can fail at; it comes in degrees, and it is a life-long moral journey of moral development (Menkiti 1984, 2004; Gyekye 1992; Wiredu 1992; Ikuenobe 2006; Behrens 2013; Oyowe 2013; Matolino 2014).

Now that we are clear regarding notions of a person in Gyekye's adumbrations, we must investigate which notion is relevant to ground human rights in moderate communitarianism. The notion that seems to be doing the work is that of moral status. Gyekye responds and criticizes Menkiti's views on ethics and politics because it operates with a conception of a person that fails to properly account for personhood, the relation between the individual and community, and the status of human rights in Afro-communitarianism. At the heart of his argument is that Menkiti holds a view that underplays or even overlooks crucial features of human nature. He agrees fully with Menkiti that personhood is relational, but he also insists that is not the whole story about personhood. In fact, Gyekye (1992) opines,

> I have made the observation that, besides being a communitarian being by nature, the human person is, also by nature, other things as well. By 'other things', I have in mind such essential attributes of the person as rationality, having a capacity for virtue and for evaluating and malting moral judgments and, hence, being capable of choice.

The view is that the relational aspect of personhood is one side of the coin. There is another side of the coin, equally definitive and essential to a correct conception of a person, the features that account for the individuality and uniqueness of a person. Gyekye refers to these individual features as "essential attributes" of our human nature. He uses words like capacities, qualities, and endowments of our nature to describe this aspect of our human nature. Gyekye points us to these features because he believes they are pointing us to the irrefutable proof of individualistic features that are necessary for human functioning and development, which a plausible political theory ought not to overlook.

Social structure is crucial, it provides both the context and resources for human development. However, it is the individualistic features of our nature that are being developed. Gyekye (1992: 111) emphasises that the community does not create these essential attributes of our nature; rather, it discovers them and has to develop them. Whereas Menkiti seemed to downplay the static isolated features of our nature, what Gyekye refers to as essential attributes, are crucial for constructing a correct approach that recognizes them and assigns them their status in a plausible conception of Afro-communitarianism.

According to Gyekye (2004: 41), therefore, a correct conception must recognize and balance the "dual features of the self". Personhood is characterized by both relational and individual features. A view of a person that accounts entirely for it in terms of social structures or community is radical and wrong-headed, According to Gyekye. A view, however, that appreciates both features of a self—individuality and relationality—is moderate and plausible. Now, we may ask, what does this moderate view of the self imply regarding human rights?

Moral Status and Human Rights

One way to construe the idea that a person is constituted by both relational and individual features may entail a conception of personal identity. It is my view. However, Gyekye aims to make more than just a claim about personal identity. He intends to make a moral claim, which will serve as a ground for human rights. To do so, he identifies that there are two moral categories related to personhood. The one moral category assigns value relative to conduct. This refers to personhood as some kind of moral achievement. Here personhood is associated with a virtuous disposition. On the other hand, Gyekye brings to our attention the category of value associated with merely possessing certain ontological features or capacities. One notion of value is agent-centred, where value emerges and tracks the quality of human effort and good character (virtue); and the other notion is patient-centred, where value is a function of a certain capacity (capacity-based approach to value) (Behrens 2013; Molefe 2024).

Whereas African scholars have been familiar with the agent-centred concept of value, it is the capacity-based concept of value that Gyekye was arguing against Menkiti's conception of personhood. It seems Menkiti did not associate intrinsic value with the capacities of our nature, or at least that was not the most important part of his moral-political theory. Hence, Menkiti's exclusive emphasis on the maximalist conception requires agents to develop and properly use these capacities. In and of themselves, it would seem, in Menkiti's view, the capacities have no intrinsic value. Gyekye's argument is precisely to point us to the idea that our capacities, or at least some of them, have intrinsic value. He makes this argument in two ways.

First, when he argues that a correct conception of a person must also come to terms with the essential attributes of the individual, his point is precisely to indicate both the instrumental and intrinsic value of these capacities. Let's focus on the intrinsic value associated with these capacities. Gyekye understands autonomy to capture the essence of our individualistic features, the essential attributes of our nature. Our individuality as persons is a function of our capacity for rationality or autonomy. He defines autonomy to refer to the human ability to self-govern or direct, which ability is directly connected to the self-determining-and-assertive aspect of human functioning (1992: 113). Gyekye (1997: 54) further informs us that "… Autonomy is …valuable in itself".

The view that autonomy as a feature of our nature is valuable in itself is philosophically significant, particularly in the context of the debate with Menkiti. First, the idea that autonomy is valuable in itself denotes that it does not derive its value by association or by use. In other words, the value associated with autonomy is the kind that it has as it is. This suggests that Gyekye believes that autonomy has intrinsic value (Korsgaard 1983). The idea of intrinsic value indicates that the source of the value in question is inherent in the thing itself. In this instance, the endowment or capacity for autonomy has intrinsic value. This idea is philosophically significant because Menkiti (and some leading scholars of African thought) tend to hold the view that none of our human capacities have intrinsic value.

Note Menkiti (2004: 326) avers, "Insofar as it [the maximalist conception of a person] reaches for something beyond such minimalist requirements as the presence of consciousness ... will ... rationality, or mental function ... *is a truly serious project that stretches beyond the raw capacities of the isolated individual*". Note also that Godfrey Tangwa (1996: 126), a leading African scholar of bioethics, opines,

> [T]he morality of an action or procedure is to be determined from the standpoint of the agent rather than that of the patient...What the attributes of self-consciousness, rationality, and freedom of choice do...is load the heavy burden of moral liability, culpability, and responsibility on the shoulders of their possessor. Human persons are not morally special; they are morally liable.

These scholars seem to think that our raw capacities or attributes load us only with moral debt, and our debt involves nurturing and developing them. In and of themselves, capacities have no intrinsic value. The bold and decisive claim of moderate communitarianism is that the individual has intrinsic value because they possess the relevant capacity. What is distinctive about moderate communitarianism is the radical claim that the individual, apart from the community, as s/he is, has value. The community has to recognize, protect, and respect this value. Respect involves both protecting the value from harm, and it also involves empowering one with such a value to lead a decent human life (Molefe 2024).

Second, Gyekye draws our attention to the intrinsic values associated with our nature by appealing to the normative concept that seems to be important in Menkiti's adumbrations. Gyekye notes the normative concept of a person, and, as explained above, he associates it with the display or practice of virtue. A person, in this normative sense, specifically the agent-centred sense, involves having a virtuous disposition. Gyekye proceeds to argue that this notion of personhood (or virtue) presupposes the capacity-based view of value, where certain capacities of our nature are intrinsically valuable. Gyekye (1992: 110) makes this argument as follows:

> The foregoing discussion ... made about the conduct of persons suggests a conception of *moral personhood*; a person is defined in terms of *moral qualities or capacities*: a human person is a being who has a moral sense and is capable of making moral judgments.

Here Gyekye derives a conception of the capacity-based view of morality from the agent-centered concept of a person. The logic is simple: the expectation that moral agents can pursue and acquire virtue presupposes that they possess capacities that can enable them to do so in the way we expect a person who has legs to be able to run. Gyekye considers these capacities to render human beings, or moral agents, morally significant in the world in a way that any entity that lacks these capacities is not. Again, it is the value associated with our moral capacities or qualities that makes Afro-communitarianism distinct from radical communitarianism.

We can now tie all of this together to an account of human rights. In Gyekye's view, a person is defined by dual features of our nature; the social/relational features and the individualistic features. The communal features correspond to the idea of the common good, which embodies an ethics of social duties. These are duties associated with recognizing, responding, and preserving relationality and communal welfare. In other words, if I am a relational creature, I work against myself if I destroy the community. To maintain my relationality, I ought to support the community by behaving in ways that promote the good of all human beings in the human community. The common good involves the state's and citizens' duties to ensure "the welfare of every member of the community". The common good refers to the basic needs that are necessary for human survival or even thriving (Gyekye 1997: 41). Hence, the relational aspect of our nature embodies a social ethics that imposes duties on the state and citizens to create conducive conditions for human functioning. Hence, Gyekye (1992: 118) remarks, "Our natural sociality then prescribes or mandates a morality that should be weighted on duty, i.e. on that which one has to do for others." The relational features of our nature orient us towards an agent-centred aspect of the moral-political theory, which specifies our duties and responsibilities towards others in the community.

The individualistic features, on the other hand, embody the idea of human dignity. To understand autonomy as a crucial feature of our nature to the point of describing it as valuable in itself suggests the idea of human dignity. Human dignity is the idea that merely because human persons possess the capacity for autonomy, they have moral worth or intrinsic value (Donnelly 1982). It is this idea of human dignity that Gyekye argues secures human rights. In fact, more carefully, it is the fact and value associated with individuality that justifies and secures a place for human rights in Afro-communitarianism. In other words, the fact that human beings have human dignity, which is a feature that does not derive from their relational nature but simply having the capacity for autonomy, means that rights are an essential and irreplaceable component of Afro-communitarianism. Human rights emerge because of human dignity, and they function essentially to protect it. Notice how Gyekye makes a connection between human dignity and human rights: "the respect for human dignity, a natural or fundamental attribute of the person … generates regard for personal rights".

In sum, Gyekye argues that any robust interpretation of Afro-communitarianism as a moral-political theory has to come to terms with the dual features of a person. It must recognize the communal features and their corresponding truck of duties to promote the welfare of every individual. It must equally recognize the individual features and their requirement to respect and protect the human dignity of each individual through the dispensation of human rights. Just as social duties to promote the common good are a natural feature of Afro-communitarianism, so are human rights a natural feature of Afro-communitarianism to protect human dignity.

To conclude a section of Gyekye's approach to human rights, note two important clarifications. First, the truckload of duties that are associated with our natural sociality are not associated with human rights at all. In Gyekye's view, these are duties that emerge as a response largely to the human condition of need, vulnerability, and insufficiency. We experience and recognize the human condition of need not in the abstract, but in the lived experience of our natural sociality. The duties in question can be associated with the responsiveness associated with caring for others with whom we share a common humanity (Gyekye 2004). Gyekye (1992: 117) informs us that "showing sensitivity to the needs of others is an important plank in the ethical platform of communitarianism". Since we share humanity in common, this fact of being social and connected with others imposes "social and ethical values of social well-being, solidarity, interdependence, cooperation, compassion, and reciprocity" as a means to sustain our common humanity (118). The first sign of moral failure is the inability to respond to the human condition of need merely because we realize that another person is in need. The ability to respond to the human condition is premised on our shared humanity.

The second consideration that flows from the one above is two-pronged. On the one hand, Afro-communitarianism tends to place a greater emphasis on duties than on human rights. The reason for this is that many of the rights, such as the "political, economic, social", would largely be catered for by a political structure that emphasizes reciprocity, interdependence, social well-being, and compassion, among others (116). The load of positive duties associated with the communitarian ethical structure already satisfies many of the human rights that individuals can claim. Moreover, Gyekye anticipates a tension between being responsive to others' needs and claiming one's rights. Concerning this tension, Gyekye (1992:115) argues that "communitarianism cannot be expected to make a fetish of rights; thus rights talk will not be brought to the front burner of its concerns and preoccupations". Instead, the communitarian system stresses the overwhelming importance of actions and values (positive duties) that seek to secure the good of all. Whereas most individualistic ethical systems will de-emphasize duties to aid others and place a prime on negative duties of protecting others from harm (Jaworska and Tannenbaum 2019). Communitarianism elevates the status of positive duties to that of negative duties. We have a stringent duty to aid or empower others, as we have to protect them from harm. It is the elevation of positive duties that justifies why Gyekye believes that individuals should not make a fetish of rights.

Lessons from the Debates on Radical and Moderate Communitarianism

The have been extensive engagements in the literature on African philosophy regarding the Menkiti-Gyekye debates on human rights (Matolino 2009, 2014; Famanikwa 2010; Metz 2012; Oyowe 2014; Molefe 2016; Ikuenobe 2018;

Chemhuru 2018). I think there are some critical lessons that we can draw from the Menkiti-Gyekye debate and the scholars who have reflected on this debate. Three lessons stand out for me (and I will not be exhaustive in my engagements with these lessons).

The Concept of a Person (Do Capacities Matter?)

In my adumbrations above, I (somewhat) indicated that there are two moral concepts of a person. I use different terms to capture these two distinct moral senses. On the one hand, we have the patient-centred notion of a person; and, on the other hand, we have the agent-centred notion of a person (Molefe 2020). The former is equivalent to the idea that ethicists describe as moral status (DeGrazia 2008; Behrens 2013). The latter is equivalent to the notion of virtue or moral excellence (Oyowe 2013). The former notion tends to focus on our capacities, the distinctive capacities that render us intrinsically valuable and, as such, make us count as proper objects of direct duties. The latter notion tends to focus on us as moral agents, bearers of responsibility, and it is a notion that tethers the agent to the community and associates virtue with a truckload of other-regarding duties. Almost all the scholars in the Menkiti-Gyekye debate are aware of this distinction, but it is never quite a direct focus of their analysis.

Typically, in the literature on human rights, human rights tend to be associated with the patient-centred notion of a person—the idea of moral status. It is the mere fact of being the kind of a thing one is—just that fact—that secures human rights. The Universal Declaration led the way in arguing that human beings have a special feature, human dignity, that justifies why we have the duty to protect their human rights. Philosophers have laboured for years to demonstrate what it is about human beings as a kind that grounds human rights. The number one candidate that scholars have tended to cite as the basis for moral status, which secures human rights, has been the ontological feature of rationality or autonomy (Miller 2017). Human rights emerge and serve to protect this distinctive human property. What secures human rights is not how one uses the property; rather, the mere possession of the property is the sufficient basis for them.

The issue in the Menkiti-Gyekye debate seems to be whether capacities can bear intrinsic value (moral status) and entail human rights (Muade 2023). Both these scholars never use the moral language of moral status, but they do use the language of human dignity, albeit they seem to have different understandings of it. Menkiti's comments on what he describes as the minimalist view of a person (which corresponds to both the idea of personal identity and/or moral status) suggest that he does not believe that the mere possession of a capacity can be a basis for moral status or intrinsic value (this view finds full and clearer expression in Polycarp Ikuenobe, whom we will consider in the next chapter at least this is my interpretation of his work). Human capacities in their raw state do not seem to bear any intrinsic value. Read in this way, it would seem Menkiti (2004: 326) does not quite subscribe to the approach to value those accounts for it in terms of moral status. The confusion, however, creeps in when Menkiti, in the context of engaging Rawls's political theory, suggests that human rights are based on moral status.

In this instance, Menkiti uses the idea of a person that sounds like moral status. Rawls, as cited by Menkiti, had argued that we owe respect to persons merely because they possess the capacity for moral personality. After citing Rawls approvingly, he makes the following observations. First, He accounts for personhood *qua* moral status in terms of the capacity for moral sense (what we may think of in terms of moral agency). Second, he states that those with this capacity are owed human rights. Third, he rejects the view that animals have rights because they lack the capacity for moral agency. Hence, it seems that the capacity for moral sense (or moral agency) is crucial for Menkiti's moral-political philosophy. What is not entirely clear, given his comments about the minimalist view of a person, however, is whether it merely has instrumental or intrinsic value.

On Gyekye's part, he argues that capacities, in and of themselves, have value—intrinsic value. Menkiti would be wrong to argue that capacities have no intrinsic value. One interesting observation regarding capacities in African philosophy seems to revolve around and affect one's conception of human rights. If one's focus is the agent-centred view of a person, moral status takes a back seat, and the focus becomes the duties towards the community. If one's focus is on moral capacities, they will insist on moral status, and human rights will feature as an important political consideration. The difference between the two scholars is that Menkiti is running with an ethical theory that associates a person with duties that are community-oriented, where capacities matter to the extent that they align with the common good. Whereas Gyekye is running with an ethical theory that seeks to balance both communal and individual duties. Hence, he ends up with a dualistic political theory that seeks to accommodate both community-oriented duties and individual-based human rights.

The Primacy of Duties

Both Menkiti and Gyekye sponsor the idea that duties are primary and human rights are secondary in Afro-communitarianism. What does this secondary ranking of human rights tell us about Afro-communitarianism? I propose that we can glean two lessons from this view. First, the ontological assumptions we make about the relationship between the individual and the community have serious consequences for human rights. Cultures that place emphasis on the community tend not to function in ways that are cognizant or place priority on human rights (see Donnelly 1982; 2009). Typically, the moral language and culture of human rights as individual entitlements/claims against others is a feature of individualistic societies like the Euro-American societies (even then, it is a modern feature of these cultures).

Second, we realize the stubbornness of the communitarian structure to accommodate human rights in a way that would satisfy scholars of human rights. Menkiti argues that personhood, ontologically and normatively, depends entirely on the community. The upshot of this view is that duties take priority over human rights. Gyekye renovates this view by balancing the individual and community, and he still ends up with a view that renders rights secondary. The point is that the moment we have an ethical theory that places the community and communal duties as part of its ethical enterprise, human rights tend to be suffocated. Gyekye is clear that in moderate communitarianism the individual is not supposed to insist or be obsessed about human rights. In the context where there is a conflict between promoting the common good and human rights, the duty to promote the common good should prevail over individual human rights. It seems the general view in Afro-communitarianism is that human rights only matter as a measure of last resort as a remedial measure where all social resources within communitarianism have failed. Where does this leave human rights—are they important at all in Afro-communitarianism?

The Normative Status of Human Rights in Afro-communitarianism

Are human rights the kinds of things that can be rendered secondary and still be relevant and powerful in a political context? In my view, scholars of African thought have tended to believe so. For example, scholars of human rights argue that what makes human rights special is their peremptory status, where they have the power (or the tendency) to set aside social goals or the common good. Though this normative status is not absolute, it is one of their defining features. In fact, Joel Feinberg (1970: 620) makes this point about human rights,

> … their [human rights] characteristic use and that for which they are distinctively well suited, is to be claimed, demanded, affirmed, insisted upon. They are especially sturdy objects to "stand upon," a most useful sort of moral furniture. Having rights, of course, makes claiming possible; but it is claiming that gives rights their special moral significance.

The defining feature of rights is that they are entitlements or claims that must be demanded and insisted upon. He uses the analogy of a moral foundation when he states they are a sturdy object to stand upon. Moreover, a moral house is empty without human rights because they are the most important moral furniture (i.e., if we want a moral home in the world, human rights provide such a place). A right-holder is, by definition, a legitimate maker of claims, and he must insist and demand that her/his rights be recognized and fulfilled.

The picture of human rights as trumps or as the kinds of claims to be demanded/insisted upon flies against the idea of rendering them secondary, as we have seen in Menkiti's and Gyekye's political theories. Human rights, as commonly understood in the Euro-American context, seem to be the kinds of political resources available to the individual to`` disrupt and compete with social goals, all things being equal. This picture of human rights brings serious challenges to both radical and moderate communitarianism. On the one hand, it seems possible to argue that the moment one assigns a secondary status to human rights, one has completely lost the plot. Human rights are important precisely because they demand primacy to protect the individual, and the most important unit in moral-political engagement is the individual. Therefore, to place the community and its good above individual rights is precisely to be against a culture of human rights, which aims to establish the priority of the individual and her own interests/good. One cannot have it both ways; one must decide where primacy lies, in the individual or community. Stated differently, one must decide how they will pursue the individual good by placing primacy on the community or the individual.

On the other hand, it could be that Donnelly (1982) and Oyowe (2013, 2014) are correct in their observation that African ethical systems are duty-based political systems. Even in instances when they seem to be calling for human rights, the language they use, and their emphasis on the community and its good, seem to point in the direction of a duty-based political theory.

Conclusion

This chapter considered the Menkiti-Gyekye debate on human rights. The chapter began by providing an exposition of Menkiti's radical communitarianism. It proceeded to elucidate Gyekye's moderate communitarianism. At the heart of this debate have been several issues. What concept of a person is relevant in the debates on human rights? The chapter indicated that there are four distinct concepts of a person, and the scholars seem to vacillate between the agent-centred (virtue) and patient-centred (moral status) notions of a person. Menkiti is more on the former, and Gyekye is more on the latter. What is the relationship between the individual and the community? Menkiti seems to believe that the community entirely defines the person, which we explained in terms of essentially shared relations, whereas Gyekye aims to balance the communal and individual features in defining a person. The upshot of this difference, we noted, on the part of Menkiti, leads to a political theory that assigns primacy to our duties towards the community, where human rights are secondary. On Gyekye's part, we recognize a political theory that seeks to assign equal status to both our duties to the collectivity and individual human rights. The latter view argues that human rights are as important as social duties.

Two issues still require further philosophical engagement in the debate on human rights in light of the Menkiti-Gyekye debate. First, scholars of African thought still need to clarify the place, status and role of capacities in ethical and political theory. Do capacities have any value at all? Are capacities morally neutral, instrumental value or intrinsically valuable? The question about the status of capacities will feature in the next chapter. Second, the question is whether we can speak meaningfully, in a politically powerful way, about human rights when salient classical theories in African philosophy can easily assign them a secondary status.

The next chapter considers the status of human rights in contemporary moral-political theorization in African philosophy.

References

Ake, C. 1987. The African Context of Human Rights. *Africa Today* 34:5–12.

Behrens, K. 2013. Two 'Normative' Conceptions of Personhood *Quest: An African. Journal of Philosophy* 25 (1–2): 103–119.

Bewaji, J., and M. Ramose. 2003. The Bewaji, Van Binsbergen and Ramose Debate On 'Ubuntu'. *South African Journal of Philosophy* 22 (4): 378–415.

Chemhuru, M. 2018. African Communitarianism and Human Rights: Towards a Compatibilist View. *Theoria* 65 (157): 37–56.

DeGrazia, D. 2008. Moral Status as a Matter of Degree? *Southern Journal of Philosophy* 46 (2): 181–198.

Donnelly, J. 1982. Human Rights and Human Dignity: An Analytic Critique of Non-Western Human Rights Conceptions. *American Political Science Review* 76:303–316.

Donnelly, J. 2009. *Human Dignity and Human Rights*. Denver: Josef Korbel School of International Studies.

Famanikwa, J. 2010. How Moderate is Kwame Gyekye's Moderate Communitarianism? *Thought and Practice: A Journal of the Philosophical Association of Kenya* 2:65–77.

Feinberg, J. 1970. The Nature and Value of Rights. *The Journal of Value Inquiry* 4:243–457.

Freeman, M. 1995. Are there Collective Human Rights? *Political Studies* 43 (1): 25–40.

Griffin, J. 2008. *On Human Rights*. Oxford: Oxford University Press.

Gyekye, K. 1992. Person and Community in African Thought. In *Person and Community: Ghanaian Philosophical Studies, 1*, ed. D. C. Washington, 101–122. Council for Research in Values and Philosophy.

Gyekye, K. 1997. *Tradition and Modernity: Philosophical Reflections on the African Experience*. New York: Oxford University Press.

Gyekye, K. 2004. *Beyond Cultures: Perceiving a Common Humanity, Ghanaian Philosophical Studies*. Accra: The Ghana Academy of Arts and Sciences.

Hughes, G. 2011. The Concept of Dignity in the Universal Declaration of Human Rights. *The Journal of Religious Ethics* 39 (1): 1–24.

Ikuenobe, P. 2006. *Philosophical Perspectives on Communalism and Morality in African Traditions*. Lanham, MD: Lexington Books.

Ikuenobe, P. 2018. Human Rights, Personhood, Dignity, and African Communalism. *Journal of Human Rights* 17 (5): 589–604.

Jaworska, A., and J. Tannenbaum. 2019. The Grounds of Moral Status. *The Stanford Encyclopedia of Philosophy*.

Kaphagawani, D. 2004. African Conceptions of a Person: A Critical Survey. In *Companion to African Philosophy*, ed. K. Wiredu, 332–442. Oxford: Blackwell.

Kittay, Eva. 2005. Equality, Dignity and Disability. In *Perspectives on Equality: The Second Seamus Heaney Lectures*, ed. M. A. Waldron and F. Lyons, 95–122. Dublin: Liffey.

Korsgaard, C. 1983. Two Distinctions in Goodness. *The Philosophical Review* 92(2):169–195.

MacIntyre, A. 1982. *After Virtue*. London: Gerald Duckworth and Co.

Matolino, B. 2009. Radicals Versus Moderates: A Critique of Gyekye's Moderate Communitarianism. *South African Journal of Philosophy* 28(2):160–170.

Matolino, B. 2014. *Personhood in African Philosophy*. Pietermaritzburg: Cluster Publications.

Mbiti, J. S. 1970. *African Religions and Philosophies*. Oxford: Heinemann.

Menkiti, I. A. 1984. Person and Community in African Traditional Thought. In *African philosophy: An introduction*, ed. R. A. Wright, 171–181. New York: University Press of America.

Menkiti, I. 2004. On the Normative Conception of Person. In *A Companion to African Philosophy*, ed. K. Wiredu, 324–331. Oxford: Blackwell.

Metz, T. 2010. Human Dignity, Capital Punishment and an African Moral Theory: Toward a New Philosophy of Human Rights. *Journal of Human Rights* 9:81–99.

Metz, T. 2012. An African Theory of Moral Status: A Relational Alternative to Individualism and Holism. *Ethical Theory and Moral Practice: An International Forum* 14:387–402.

Metz, T. 2013. Introduction: Engaging with the Philosophy of D. A. Masolo. *Quest* 25:7–17.
Miller, S. 2017. Reconsidering Dignity Relationally. *Ethics and Social Welfare* 11:108–121.
Molefe, M. 2016. Revisiting the Gyekye-Menkiti Debate: Who is a Radical Communitarian? *Theoria* 63 (149): 37–54.
Molefe, M. 2017. Personhood and Rights in an African Tradition. *Politikon* 45(2):217–231.
Molefe, M. 2019. *An African Philosophy of Personhood, Morality and Politics*. New York, NY: Palgrave Macmillan.
Molefe, M. 2020. Solving the Conundrum of African Philosophy Through Personhood: The Individual or Community? *Journal of Value Inquiry* 54(1):41–57.
Molefe, M. 2021. *Partiality and Impartiality in African Philosophy*. Lanham, MD: Lexington Books.
Molefe, M. 2024. *Ubuntu, Umuntu and Human Dignity*. Ubuntu: Interdisciplinary Conversations Across Continents.
Muade, E. 2023. Moderate Communitarianism and Human Dignity. In *Human Dignity in an African Context*, ed. E. Pellegrino, 107–126. New York, NY: Palgrave Macmillan.
Neal, P., and D. Paris. 1990. Liberalism and the Communitarian Critique: A Guide for the Perplexed. *Canadian Journal of Political Science/Revue canadienne de science politique* 23(3):419–439.
Oyowe, A. 2013. Personhood and Social Power in African Thought. *Alternation (Durban)* 20:203–228.
Oyowe, A. 2014. Fiction, Culture, and the Concept of a Person. *Research in African Literatures* 45 (2): 46–62.
Oyowe, O. A. 2022. *Menkiti's Moral Man*. New York: Lexington Books.
Tangwa, G. 1996. Bioethics: An African Perspective. *Bioethics* 10:183–200.
Warren, A. 1997. *Moral Status: Obligations to Persons and Other Living Things*. Oxford: Clarendon Press.
Wiredu, K. 1992. Moral Foundations of an African Culture. In *Person and Community: Ghanaian Philosophical Studies*, ed. K. Wiredu and K. Gyekye, 193–206. Washington, DC: The Council for Research in Values and Philosophy.
Wiredu, K. 1996. *Cultural Universals and Particulars: An African Perspective*. Indianapolis: Indiana University Press.
Wiredu, K. 2009. An Oral Philosophy of Personhood: Comments on Philosophy and Orality. *Research in African Literatures* 40(1):8–18.

Chapter 3
Contemporary Theories of Human Rights in African Philosophy

Introduction

This chapter provides an overview of contemporary theories of human rights in African philosophy. It will focus on three theories from scholars working in African moral-political thought, namely, (a) the (moral) status (Metz 2011), (b) the personhood-based (Ikuenobe 2018), and (c) the recognition theories of human rights (Allsobrook 2023). I describe these theories as 'contemporary' because they were developed in a generation after the one of the scholars who pioneered the philosophical discussions around the theme of personhood and human rights in African philosophy—the classical theories are dated roughly from the late 1970s to 1999, and the contemporary ones are from the year 2000.[1] The contemporary theories of human rights are an outgrowth, a response, and a continuation of the pioneers' initial contribution to the conversations and debates on human rights in African philosophy. The previous chapter explored how scholars in the classical period contributed to human rights. This chapter philosophically considers how scholars in the contemporary period have advanced the conversation about the place, relevance, and meaning of human rights in African philosophy.

The three theories that we will consider share one thing in common—they all endorse the view that human rights are relevant and have a place in a robust interpretation of African political thought. It is crucial to observe, however, that they do so in different ways. For example, the debates on human rights between radical and moderate communitarianism pivoted on the idea of personhood. The idea of personhood still features as a significant component of human rights even among contemporary scholars of human rights. They differ, however, in terms of how they

[1] I stipulate the terms and historical classification—'classical' and 'contemporary'—to distinguish one generation of scholars from another in the development of ideas in African philosophy. The terms and classification are for convenience and heuristic purposes to facilitate a meaningful conversation about the development of ideas in African philosophy.

M. Molefe, *An Introduction to Human Rights in African Philosophy*, SpringerBriefs in Ethics, https://doi.org/10.1007/978-3-032-04447-1_3

understand the concept of personhood and how this concept relates to human rights. The (moral) status view of human rights grounds the entire moral edifice that justifies them (human rights) on the basis of human capacities, specifically the capacity for friendliness (Metz 2022). On the status view, the ontological make-up of persons (their capacities in their raw state and undeveloped state) are necessary and sufficient grounds for human dignity and human rights. The personhood-based view of human rights, on the other hand, insists that human capacities are necessary but not sufficient for human rights. In fact, it is the actual development and proper use of capacities that grounds human dignity and human rights (Ikuenobe 2017).

The moral status view and the personhood-based view, in a crucial way, may be construed as a continuation of the debate between radical and moderate communitarianism, where both clarify and bolster the views of classical theorists. The moral status view endorses and amends the moderate communitarianism that insists that capacities are the basis for human dignity, and the personhood-based view clarifies and defends radical communitarianism that insists that it is the actual use of our capacities that secures human dignity and rights.[2] Whereas the moral status and personhood-based views of human rights pivot on the idea of personhood, the recognition theory of human rights breaks new ground by insisting that human rights have nothing to do with the essential ontological capacities of our nature or their actualization. Instead, it insists that human rights are customary practices among all cultures, African cultures included, that serve as an attempt to capture the common good on the basis of our shared humanity (Allsobrook 2023). On this view, human rights are contingent features of our political cultures to recognize and protect human dignity that is a function of our shared lived experience of struggling and resisting suffering oppression and threats posed by modern human conditions of existence.

The chapter will proceed by considering the three theories of human rights, respectively. I urge the reader to keep the following considerations in mind when engaging with this chapter. The aim of this chapter (even this book) is to provide an introductory overview of the conversations and debates on human rights. This stated purpose has several implications. The book does not aim to defend or advance any novel views about human rights in African philosophy. The purpose of the book is merely expository or interpretive. I will provide, to the best of my abilities, the ideas and arguments marshalled by the theorists of human rights to give the reader a picture of the debates on human rights in African philosophy. Another scholar may have chosen different scholars, but I chose these as they seem to be somewhat

[2] Though the status view endorses moderate communitarianism, it differs significantly from it in terms of the account it provides for moral status. The status view grounds moral status on the capacity for friendliness, whereas Gyekye grounds it on the capacity for autonomy. They also differ regarding how they account for relationality (importance of relationships) in their moral-political accounts. The personhood-based view essentially attempts to both clarify and augment some of the ideas associated with radical communitarianism. It augments Menkiti's conception of human dignity and (it can read) as an attempt to justify why human rights are secondary in African political thought.

interesting and salient in the tradition of African philosophy. Moreover, they all approach the conversation on human rights from the same starting point—the Menkiti-Gyekye conversation in African philosophy that has shaped much of contemporary African moral-political philosophy.

Below, I offer a philosophical exposition of the (moral) status view of human rights.

The Moral Status Theory of Human Rights[3]

This chapter expounds on the moral status view of human rights. I associate the moral status view of human rights in African philosophy with Thaddeus Metz, who has made a significant contribution to African moral-political thought. Metz grounds his moral-theoretical contributions on the indigenous concept of Ubuntu (see 2007a, 2010, 2011, 2012a). The Nguni concept of Ubuntu embraces an African worldview, or even a philosophy comprising metaphysics, epistemology, and axiology (Ramose 1999; Shutte 2001; Nkondo 2007; Behrens 2011; Dladla 2017; Molefe 2024). Cultural insiders and scholars explain the essence of Ubuntu by invoking the proverb 'Umuntu ngumuntu ngabantu' (in isiZulu), 'Motho ke motho ka batho' (in seSotho), 'A person is a person through other persons.' The proverb does have ontological implications that point to a relational conception of reality, where the entire realm of existence (the natural and supernatural) and what it means to be human cannot be adequately and correctly captured without accentuating relationships as a point of departure (Louw 2004; Menkiti 2004; Metz 2007a). However, it is the normative implications of this proverb that are generally important in Metz's African moral-political theorization (Metz 2007a).

To navigate our journey to Metz's theory of human rights. We will begin by understanding his moral theory i.e., how he accounts for the good or right action. We will take special notice of the two distinct theories of right action in his moral theorization—one accounts for the good or right action in terms of the *actual* friendly relations themselves and another in terms of the *capacity* for such friendly relations. The latter view is tantamount to his account of moral status and/or human dignity, which serves as the ground for human rights. Finally, we will consider his account of human rights.

---

[3]I am aware that describing Metz's theory of human rights as a 'status' approach to them may mislead some thinkers to associate his approach to a certain approach to them in the Euro-American tradition (see Waldron 2012). On this view, status refers to a membership or position, and to have such a status amounts to "particular package of rights, powers, disabilities, duties, privileges, immunities, and liabilities accruing to a person by virtue of the condition or situation they are in" (2012: 24). On this view, status has nothing to do with our ontological make-up or some intrinsic capacities. I use the idea of status, when I explain Metz's view, to refer or track the idea of moral status, which is a function of possession certain intrinsic features (Behrens 2013).

Metz's Moral Theory

The proverb 'A person is a person through other persons' signals the importance of social relationships in accounting for morality in African ethics. In fact, this proverb could be interpreted to suggest that the entire enterprise of morality is essentially constituted by some way of interacting and connecting with others in relationships (Metz 2012b). Scholars of African thought, including Metz, have instances in their writings where they advocate for a relational interpretation of African ethics. Note that Nhlanhla Mkhize (2008: 38–39) commenting on the psychology and ontology informing African moral thought, observes that the "ideal (the good) is an ordered or balanced state of affairs; human wrongdoing, unethical conduct or social injustice destabilizes this order". For another, Anne Verhoef and Michel (1997: 395, emphasis mine) apprises us that African thought "places a high value on harmonious human relations which link people together in a collective existence through an interconnected web.". They proceed to remark that "cooperation and social harmony are valued over competition and individualism" (ibid.). Desmond Tutu (1999: 35), famous for chairing the South African Truth and Reconciliation Commission, remarks as follows regarding Ubuntu—

> When we want to give high praise to someone we say, "Yu, u nobuntu"; "Hey, so-and-so has ubuntu." Then you are generous, you are hospitable, you are friendly and caring and compassionate. You share what you have. . . . Harmony, friendliness, community are great goods. Social harmony is for us the summum bonum—the greatest good.

The recurrent theme from these scholars is that morality revolves around social relationships that connect or bind people together. Scholars of African thought tend to account for the morally relevant connections/relationships between people in terms of the value of social harmony. Tutu above goes to the extent of describing social harmony as the greatest good in African ethics. In this relational interpretation of African ethics, social harmony is the highest good, and division is the worst moral evil. It is the moral insight regarding the intrinsic or high value placed on social harmony that is recurrent in African cultures that underscores Metz's own interpretation of Ubuntu. In fact, Metz is overt that he draws his inspiration to espouse a relational interpretation of Ubuntu, which posits social harmony as the highest good, from Tutu's adumbrations on it (Jones and Metz 2015). Metz, however, intervenes in the relational interpretation of African ethics by philosophically teasing out the normative content of social harmony.

In my interpretation of Metz's moral theory, I identify two ways to interpret to the value of social harmony as a moral theory. One interpretation is teleological and another deontological. The teleological moral theory of Ubuntu posits that the promotion of actual harmonious relations constitutes what morality is all about. For example, Metz (2007a: 331) distinguishes between individualistic and collectivistic (or communitarian) theories of value. The former accounts for the good in terms of some property of the individual like, pleasure, and the latter on the actual relationships (Metz 2014). Initially, Metz accounted for morality in terms of the latter—morality resides in actual relationships (see Metz 2007b, 2010, 2016). The deontological interpretation, on the other hand, among others, locates the good in our capacity to participate in social relationships, and not the relationship itself (see 2010, 2011, 2012a,b, 2022).

Before we can zoom into the distinction between these two ways of accounting for the good/right action in Metz's moral theory. We first need to clarify how Metz construes the value of social harmony that lies at the heart of African moral thought. Metz observes that scholars have not always been very clear and precise regarding what social harmony means in a way that can make it a meaningful moral theory in terms of guiding conduct. He provides his own philosophical exposition to render the value and relationship of social harmony precise enough to guide conduct. In his interpretation, social harmony comprises two distinct social relationships, namely, *social identity* and *solidarity* (or goodwill) (Metz 2007b, 2014).

The relationship of social identity comprises three elements. First, the individual conceives of her personal identity in terms of we rather than I. In other words, the individual conceives of her own identity in terms of being connected with others. The connection with others is ideally reciprocal (i.e., those with whom she is connected must also think of the individual as part of the group). The second component of social identity is the idea that those who are in a 'we-relationship' have common goals and aspirations. Finally, they also collaborate and jointly pursue their shared aspirations and goals. On the other hand, solidarity involves an attitude and conduct characterized by empowering others. The empowerment in question involves other-regarding duties motivated by empathy or even sympathy to enhance the humanity and objective well-being of another person. In sum, social identity involves "sharing a way of life" and solidarity "caring about their quality of life" for their own sakes (Metz 2011: 539).

In short, social harmony involves the *sharing* and *caring* components. These two components cover both the attitudes and behaviours associated with social harmony (Metz 2013). On the one hand, social harmony involves a positive connection with others. On the other hand, it involves empowering those with whom one connects. Metz informs us that these two may go apart, conceptually and in practice. In the one scenario, we have sharing without caring. An example of this according to him, is a typical capitalist firm, where employees of a company like MTN share a sense of being a part of a group and coordinate their behaviour to offer a service but often have instances of lack of solidarity (or care) with management over salary disputes (Metz 2007a). An instance of care without sharing occurs when one donates money to a charity to provide food for those starving in Somalia. In caring without sharing, there is no connection between the benefactor and recipient; there is just a caring sentiment and action designed to alleviate poverty. Metz insists, however, that social harmony fully occurs when the two—sharing and caring—are conjoined together (2007a, 2017, 2022).

To illuminate what sharing and caring involve, they may be viewed as kinds of loving and friendly relations (Metz 2007a). Both these relationships have the aspect of identifying with another in the context of a 'we' and the element of empowering or improving another's welfare for their own sake. In his recent writings, he speaks more carefully of friendliness (Metz 2022). For him, friendliness is a technical moral term that captures the essence of African moral thought *qua* social harmony (which comprises sharing and caring). Metz makes two crucial points regarding how we should understand the relational value of friendliness. First, Metz (2022: 96) clarifies, "I expect that such a word (friendliness) will connote less emotional intensity to readers, while capturing the key elements of a sense of togetherness, cooperative interaction, aid, and sympathetic altruism". Second, Metz (2022: 157) distinguishes friendship and friendliness, and he grounds right action on the latter. For him, friendship is too demanding to be a ground for a moral theory since it "involves longer and stronger bonds" that are not necessary to capture the morally relevant sense of social harmony (ibid.). He argues that we are not required to become friends with others, but morality essentially pivots on "prizing friendliness … A friendly way of relating", which is distinct from "a full-blown relationship" (ibid.). He believes that the typical social relationships we have with our neighbours, colleagues at work, and fellow church members, relationships in professional associations, characteristically embody friendly and intuitively desirable ways of relating without necessarily being full-blown relationships of friendship.

In sum, for Metz, all that friendliness should embody is a value that can be expected to guide how we relate to all moral patients. In this light, friendship will be a tall order as the basis for a moral theory or to capture social harmony. Rather, it is the technical notion of friendliness, which merely requires moral agents to prize friendly relations or to treat others with friendliness (without necessarily being friends with them). Friendliness embodies an attitude and conduct that highly values sharing and caring as a proper way to relate and engage with others (which is different from being friends with them).

Now that we are clear regarding Metz's interpretation of social harmony in terms of friendliness, we proceed to note two distinct moral theories in his moral philosophy. In his initial moral theorization, Metz accounts for the rightness of actions in terms of prizing friendly relations themselves—a right action has the property of properly relating with others by prizing friendly relations (Metz 2011, 2012a). It is the actual relationship of friendliness that captures the essence of morality. On this view, Metz is very clear that we relate to the value of friendliness by prizing it rather than promoting it. The distinction between prizing (honouring) and promoting has serious philosophical implications.[4] The former signals a moral theory that takes a deontological posture (i.e., our duty revolves around respecting the value in question even if doing so may lead to there being less of it). The latter takes a teleological posture (i.e., our duty involves making sure that there is as much friendliness as possible even if we can achieve it by deploying unfriendly means). In his first

[4] McNaughton and Rawling (1992) in the essay "Honoring and Promoting Values" draws a distinction regarding how to relate to a value. Promoting a value involves ensuring that there is as much of it as is possible in the world, even if that requires violating or undermining the value in question. If by cheating on my wife, there will be more loyalty in the world, then I have a duty to cheat. Honoring a value involves respecting the single instance of the value in question even if doing so would mean there is less of it in the world. I must be loyal to my wife even if doing so may lead her to being unfaithful.

writing, Metz gave a teleological picture of African ethics (see Metz 2007a,b), but indicated that he did not even at that time think it was adequate (e.g. 2007a, 338). In his latter writings, Metz defends a certain deontological interpretation of African ethics (Metz 2022).

In his latter writings (we are now moving to his second way of accounting for African ethics), Metz abandons the view that it is friendliness itself that accounts for the right actions or the good. Instead, he grounds it on the capacity for friendliness. In his moral philosophy, he relates to the capacity for friendliness in two different ways. On the one hand, he presents it as a theory of right action, wherein a right action is a function of respecting the capacity for friendliness (Metz 2010, 2011). If there is an object, be it a human being, that has the said capacity, the right action involves respecting the human being merely because s/he possesses the relevant capacity. On the other hand, the capacity for friendliness features as a theory of moral status and/or human dignity (see Metz 2010, 2011, 2022). A more accurate rendition, however, would suggest that it is human dignity *qua* the capacity for friendliness that simultaneously accounts for the rightness of actions. Hence, Metz (2010: 94) would express his moral theory in this fashion—

> U2: An act is wrong (at least in part) because it degrades the individual's dignity that she has in virtue of her capacity to engage in harmonious relationships.

The capacity for friendliness is tantamount to an account of human dignity. So far, we have noted two distinct principles of right action or the good. The one principle entirely accounts for the right action in terms of promoting/prizing social relationships of friendliness. The latter view grounds it strictly on respecting the capacity for friendliness. We note that Metz introduces the idea of human dignity in relation to the latter rendition of his theory, where it is a function of possessing the capacity for friendliness. It is the idea of human dignity that will help us understand Metz's approach to human rights.

Below, I will explore the relationship between moral status, human dignity, and human rights in Metz's moral philosophy.

Moral Status, Human Dignity and Human Rights

At the heart of Metz's approach to human dignity is a relationship between moral status, human dignity, and human rights. It is our status of dignity that qualifies us for human rights, and human rights function precisely to protect our status of dignity. To get a grip on this view of human rights, we need to understand the relationship between these three concepts, namely, moral status, human dignity, and human rights. It is the capacity for friendliness that captures human dignity. The idea of human dignity expresses a special value associated with the being under consideration. This special value is often expressed in terms of moral worth or moral preciousness (Donnelly 2015). We can imagine the specialness of the value associated with human dignity in three ways.

First, the possession of the capacity for friendliness renders us morally special and distinct in a way that beings that lack this feature are not. The ontological make-up of the capacity for friendliness requires that we be regarded and treated in a special way. Second, the value associated with human dignity is usually expressed in terms of it being intrinsic rather than extrinsic (Sulmasy 2008; Hughes 2011). Intrinsic value is the kind of value that is inborn, inherent (i.e., it is a kind of value that is a function of the natural endowment of the being in question), and it is superlative (Sulmasy 2008). Thus, when we speak of human dignity, we speak of a dignity that we have because we possess certain value-endowing ontological features, specifically, the capacity for friendliness. It is the possession of the relevant ontological capacities, and not their use, which secures human dignity. Hence, accounting for the value associated with dignity implies that it is the kind of value that is inborn, which implies that we do not derive it from any external factor, nor do we earn it (Hughes 2011). Just being born with the relevant ontological feature is sufficient for human dignity. Moreover, there is nothing that we can do to obliterate our human dignity—it is not a merit term.

Secondly, some scholars interpret human dignity by appealing to the analogy of height (Rosen 2012). When they think of it in this fashion, they tend to frame it along the rubric of a hierarchy. In terms of the analogy of a hierarchy, human dignity refers to the highest value—it is the value that corresponds to occupying the apex position in the hierarchy (a superlative value). Analogizing human dignity with a hierarchy has interesting implications to the effect that there may be other beings with value, albeit inferior or below the one associated with human dignity that corresponds to the highest position, the apex (Toscano 2011). In Metz's approach, at least how I think it is best construed his ethical theory, it is the language of moral status that best helps us to understand the idea of a human being as the possessor of superlative value in the hierarchy.

The idea of moral status refers to direct objects of moral obligations (Reichlin 2014). The objects of direct moral obligations have inherent value (DeGrazia 2008). Hence, moral agents owe them direct moral obligations. The obligations in question can both be negative and positive (Metz 2012a). Obligations are negative in as far as moral agents have a duty not to harm a bearer of moral status, and they are positive in as far as they involve empowering beings of moral status. What connects the idea of moral status with human dignity is that moral status comes in degrees, where some beings have lower, and others have it in higher degrees. In other words, the urgency and stringency of duties towards a particular being that has moral status depends on the degree to which it has moral status (Jaworska and Tannenbaum 2023). Human dignity understood within a framework of moral status refers to the highest level of moral status. To claim that human beings have dignity is tantamount to the view that they occupy the highest moral status, at least when we are in a position to affect them.

To have moral status, or human dignity, has implications regarding how one should be treated. Throughout his writings, Metz defends the idea that human beings, as bearers of moral status, or human dignity, ought to be treated in a particular way (Metz 2012a). For example, so far as I am aware, the first essay by Metz that introduced his conception of human dignity *qua* the capacity for friendliness, its focus was on the question of the permissibility of capital punishment (Metz 2010). Put simply, the argument was that it is impermissible, or even degrading, to subject bearers of human dignity to capital punishment. Capital punishment, say, for a murder that has already been committed, is wrong because it undermines their capacity for friendliness or human dignity, whereas, Metz maintains, the use of deadly force to prevent a murder would not be degrading in that way. In other words, the insight that emerges is that the status of human dignity entails certain (negative) rights, which are quite stringent. In this instance, the state has a duty not to subject its citizens to capital punishment. Human rights, therefore, are a function of the status of human dignity, and they function to protect this valuable status of dignity. Note this comment by Manuel Toscano (2011), which I believe helps us to understand Metz's approach to moral status and human rights:

> Hence the close link we assume between status and rights. That way it is easy to think about the latter as a sort of boundary or "protective perimeter"... Indeed, this protective perimeter delineates the idea of personal inviolability guaranteed by rights that contemporary authors identify with the very concept of moral status... So, the higher the status, the greater and the stronger will be the protective perimeter, namely the number and stringency of rights ensuring the inviolability of the holder.

In his analysis, Metz begins by delineating the status of human dignity associated with human beings. Human beings have the highest moral status or human dignity, because they possess the capacity for friendliness, both as a subject and an object, meaning that it is both their ability to be friendly towards others and to be befriended by them that counts. It is the possession of moral status that secures the protective parameter within which the possessor of the status is guaranteed rights that protect their inviolability. Note the following sentiments expressed by Metz (2011) that endorse or suggest a moral status approach to human rights. In the essay 'Ubuntu as a moral theory and human rights in South Africa,' Metz states, "One has a human right to something... because of some quality one shares with (nearly) all other human beings and that must be fulfilled..." (541). Having a right is a function of possessing some quality, and it is the possession of this quality that requires the fulfilment of a right. In other words, it is the possession of the quality of the capacity to be a party to friendly ways of relating that secure human rights, and which rights must be fulfilled because of this ontological fact (or quality of our nature). In the same essay, he states, "I assume that to observe human rights is to treat an individual as having a dignity, roughly, as exhibiting a superlative non-instrumental value" (ibid., 542). Rights aim to recognize and protect human dignity.

In this view, human rights serve to protect human dignity *qua* the capacity for friendliness. There are two related implications from this way of understanding human rights. On the one hand, human rights expressed positively serve to preserve or enhance the human capacity for friendliness. In this light, human rights are enablers of our humanity in as far as they empower us with freedoms, liberties, and opportunities to develop or nurture that which captures the essence of our humanity. On the other hand, human rights expressed negatively serve to protect us from "extraordinary forms of unfriendliness" designed to deny, degrade, or even erase our sense of humanity (Metz 2011: 545), which, according to Metz, degrade our ability to be an object of friendly relations. Hence, Ubuntu offers an account of human rights understood within the relational frame of friendliness, where they serve to protect and enhance our capacity to share and care for others and to be shared with and cared for by others. Human rights are moral instruments for creating a friendly moral-political culture on the part of the state, whereas human rights violations create a culture of extraordinary unfriendliness. A socially just society creates a conducive environment for friendliness to thrive.

The friendliness view of human rights provides a relational interpretation of human rights violation. Rape is a human rights violation because it undermines one as the object of friendly relations. As objects of friendly relations, we are the kinds of beings that can be interacted with and corporated with, but rape essentially denies this crucial feature of our humanity in that way undermining our human rights. This view is distinct from the typical Euro-Americal view of autonomy, where rape is a human rights violation because the victim is treated merely as a means. What is at issue regarding the friendliness view when rights are violated is our special social nature to be a part of corporative engagements such as sexual engagements.

In sum, the moral status view regards human rights to be a function of protecting our capacity for friendliness. The entire franchise of human rights imagines a socially just society as one that creates conditions generally conducive to friendliness. Human rights respect the human capacity for friendliness.

Next, we turn to Polycarp Ikuenobe's conception of human rights.

Personhood-Based Theory of Human Rights

This section considers Polycarp Ikuenobe's theory of human rights. Two essays will be crucial to offer what I consider to be Ikuenobe's account of human rights, namely, 'The Communal Basis for Moral Dignity: An African Perspective' (2017) and 'Human Rights, Personhood, Dignity, and African Communalism' (2018). In these two essays, he clearly and probably fully lays out his conception of African ethical and political theory. In the first essay, he accounts for human dignity by invoking Menkiti's rendition of the African concept of personhood. In the second essay, he grounds human dignity and human rights on the same concept of personhood. In the second essay, he explicitly states, "I accept Menkiti's account of personhood, and [I] use it as a foundation for a plausible African conception of dignity and human rights" (2018: 589). On the same page, he promises in this essay "to articulate a plausible conception of substantive human rights that is grounded in an African communal conception of dignity and personhood that emphasizes individual responsibility" (ibid.).

One of the things that emerges from Ikuenobe's approach to human rights is that he builds on a distinctive African conception of personhood. The same notion of personhood also grounds his conception of human dignity. If one takes seriously the last quotation above, it reads as if Ikuenobe's conception of human rights is grounded on two distinct grounds: 'an African communal conception of dignity *and* personhood that emphasizes individual responsibility.' In what follows below, I want to provide an outline and exposition of both of these concepts—personhood and dignity—which I believe will bring us closer to his conception of what he calls "substantive human rights." I will indicate that moral personhood is equivalent to moral dignity (2018: 589). By 'substantive human rights,' he intends to distinguish his own view from the standard and influential account of them that tends to regard them as individual self-regarding entitlements without regard to the human community (social-moral interactions that provide a context for human survival and thriving). According to him, substantive human rights must be imagined within a community that provides socio-cultural and political resources and opportunities that enable citizens to make "socio-moral-legal claims" (2018: 600).

I begin below with the outline and exposition of the concepts of a person in Ikuenobe's political philosophy.

The Concept of a Person in Ikuenobe's Moral Philosophy

Throughout his writings, Ikuenobe distinguishes the metaphysical and normative (moral) concepts of a person (2006, 2015, 2016, 2018, 2023). This is really a distinction between the fact of being human with particular ontological features, such as a body, soul, and psychological capacities, and what a human being achieves, as the moral agent, in the socio-moral domain, which scholars typically capture in terms of virtue or excellence (see Menkiti 1984, 2004; Oyowe 2013; Behrens 2013; Molefe 2019). The one notion of a person is a biological given; we are born with it as a species: we are born with particular features or capacities that are definitive of our ontological kind (Ikuenobe 2023). The other notion of a person is not a given; we must strive for it; we earn it relative to the quality of our actions, conduct, and character. It is the development and use of our capacities, in a social context, that earns us the status of a person. Put simply, when we are born, we are simply human with the capacity to become persons (a moral agent that has achieved a virtuous character disposition).

The distinction is crucial in Menkiti's and Ikuenobe's moral-political philosophy. Menkiti (1984: 172) captures this distinction in terms of the *minimalist* and the *maximalist* conception of a person. He associates the former with the Euro-American conception of a person. According to Menkiti (1984: 173), the minimalist view defines a person with reference to particular ontological and/or psychological capacities such as "soul, or rationality, or will, or memory." In contrast, Menkiti (1984: 173) postulates an African conception of a person that he describes as maximalist, which construes personhood as a moral goal that moral agents can be "competent or ineffective, better or worse" at depending on the quality of their conduct. According to Menkiti, as much as individual effort is crucial, it must be appreciated in the context of the support that the community provides via "the rituals of incorporation" that are crucial for being socialized and internalizing "the social rules by which the community lives" (ibid.). The internalization of the social rules of the community, when successfully coupled with moral compliance, would amount to a socio-moral transformation of what "was initially biologically given ...[to]... become a person with all the inbuilt excellencies implied by the term" (1984: 173).

Several things stand out about this conception of a person. First, it is not sufficient to merely define personhood in terms of our ontological capacities. Ontological capacities are mere instruments for human functioning, survival, or even thriving. In fact, Ikuenobe (2023: 48) states, "one's capacity is a 'tool,' a 'potentiality' to be developed...". It is how we use these tools that make all the moral difference in terms of moral development or personhood. Personhood involves human effort to be better or worse (i.e., social-moral character development or deterioration). Personhood indicates a socio-moral status that comes in degrees, where one could either have less or more of it and even the possibility of not having it at all. African moral cultures aim to educate and empower the moral agent to become a person (virtuous). It does so through socio-communal resources, which provide opportunities and processes through which one could learn crucial social, cultural, and moral rules to be an effective member of the community and to contribute to its well-being and thereby attain the status of personhood (Gyekye 1997). Essentially, the rituals of incorporation involve the provision of resources to empower what was merely a biological being to become a moral being, a bearer of excellence (Menkiti 2004). In another place, Menkiti refers to this process of converting what was merely a human being to become a person in terms of the "in-gathering of excellences" (2004: 325).

In light of Menkiti's conception of a person, Ikuenobe further clarifies this view by highlighting four crucial features of it. First, he endorses Menkiti's adumbration of the African person as constituted by both the factual (metaphysical feature of our human nature) and the moral/normative aspects of it, which involves the participation in a communal context, the acquisition of virtue/excellence, and promoting the communal welfare. Second, the ontological features of a person, as captured by the minimalist definition, what Menkiti (2004: 325) refers to as "the raw capacities of the isolated individual", in and of themselves, have no intrinsic value. Capacities have instrumental value (Ikuenobe 2017). Genuine value, rather than mere instrumental value, emerges relative to the use and development of the ontological capacities. The development and use of the ontological features is tantamount to the achievement or earning the status of personhood. In other words, the insight here is that African personhood is a merit and virtue concept, which refers to a moral agent that has nurtured their capacities in the communal context, and s/he is using them to contribute to the social well-being of the community.

The third insight that emerges in Ikuenobe's (2017: 441) analysis is that we regard the concept of a person as a thick concept. He comments as follows regarding the thick concept as it relates to personhood:

> ... with both descriptive and evaluative components, and that both components are essential for understanding it [personhood]. The descriptive component indicates some factual metaphysical, psychological, and spiritual features ... such as freewill, mind, soul, vitality, agency, and the normative component...

Whereas Menkiti may be construed as merely distinguishing the factual and moral aspects of a person, as in the minimalist and maximalist conception of a person, Ikuenobe insists that a correct way to read Menkiti requires that we understand both aspects to be part of a plausible conception of a person. For conceptual clarity and philosophical elucidation, we may speak of these—the factual and normative—as distinct concepts. However, if we aim to give a complete picture of personhood, we have to understand them as conjoined. Hence, Ikuenobe (2017: 446) states, "The normative conception of personhood depends on the existence of the requisite descriptive features.".

The major takeaway from this conception of personhood is twofold. On the one hand, ontological capacities have no intrinsic value. Instead, it is the insistence of Ikuenobe that they only have instrumental value (Ikuenobe 2017). On the other hand, one attains personhood relative to the internalization and acquisition of social and developmental parts of their ontological capacities to be characterized by virtue or excellence—personhood is possible only in the context of a community. Armed with this understanding of personhood, we can turn to Ikuenobe's conception of human dignity, as it will lead us to his conception of human rights.

Ikuenobe on Human Dignity

I make three crucial observations regarding human dignity in Ikuenobe's moral-political philosophy. First, Ikuenobe distinguishes between *factual* and *moral* dignity. One has factual dignity relative to whether s/he possesses the relevant ontological features, such as "vitality, life, soul, breathe, or spirit, and the capacity for cognition, rationality, autonomy…" (2017: 457). As human beings, we have factual dignity because we possess the metaphysical capacities associated with our nature. On the other hand, moral dignity refers to moral achievements that have to do with the quality of our comportment, character and contribution to social welfare and harmony. Ikuenobe (2018: 603) informs us that "moral dignity is … manifested in the active and positive actions that indicate self-respect, respect for, and responsibility to, others". In another place, he notes that "Moral dignity involves a normative evaluative judgment about someone based on the moral quality of her character, achievement, comportment, or behaviour". We have the former by nature, or since we have the relevant ontological features. We achieve the latter relative to the quality of our actions and character. It is the latter that he uses to ground human dignity.

Second, Ikuenobe claims that he grounds human dignity on the normative concept of a person (i.e., personhood is the basis for human dignity). I suggest that a plausible way to interpret Ikuenobe involves understanding him to be saying that the African concept of personhood has its own way of accounting for human dignity. In other words, a careful exposition of the factual and moral facets of personhood provides us with the corresponding factual and moral components of human dignity. The former is universal since it applies to all human beings since they possess the relevant metaphysical capacities (and only secures factual human dignity), and the latter is merit-based as it relates to and identifies moral agents that develop and positively use their metaphysical capacities (moral dignity is a status we earn relative to the quality of our conduct) to bear virtue. In fact, a more careful reading would suggest that the normative concept of personhood embodies or is equivalent to moral dignity.

Throughout his discussion of the concepts of a person and human dignity, he uses language that suggests that they are one and the same concept. For example, he talks of "morally ascribing or denying personhood or dignity and then respect by others" as if personhood and dignity are interchangeable (2017: 446). Also note that personhood is something that can be denied as is dignity—note, it is moral dignity that can be denied, and not the factual one. The same logic of treating these concepts as if they are the same manifests in these quotes, "Personhood and dignity are not simply the mere having of metaphysical capacities, but how well morally one uses one's metaphysical capacities" (2018: 591). Both concepts involve moral experience associated with the positive use of our ontological capacities. In another place, "... one cannot be called a person or dignified if one has not satisfied the normative criteria (2017: 446). Finally, Ikuenobe avers that the statement that one "'is not a person', or 'has no moral dignity'... is a moral ascription based on a normative judgment, which is that one has good character, behaved morally... (ibid.,).

The reader is left with two options regarding the relationship between personhood and moral dignity. It is either both concepts refer to the same metaphysical capacities, whose positive use amounts to personhood and/or moral dignity (the two concepts are the same) or there are different or distinct metaphysical capacities in human beings, whose development and positive use amount to different moral experiences—one related to personhood and another to human dignity. The latter view strikes me as implausible, hence I believe that the normative notion of a person is tantamount to moral dignity. The pursuit of personhood is tantamount to the acquisition of moral dignity. To acquire personhood means that the agent is leading a dignified life.

Finally, for Ikuenobe, human dignity, specifically, moral dignity is a moral experience that depends on our conduct. We achieve moral dignity in the context of human interaction in the community. We earn moral dignity relative to being responsive to the community and its needs. The exercise of responsibilities that promote the common good earns us moral dignity. Hence, Ikuenobe (2023: 49, emphasis mine) would opine, "Therefore, *moral dignity* and correlative honour and respect by others are *earned* and *deserved*". In this view, human dignity *qua* moral dignity is conditional and alienable. The condition for deserving the status of human dignity and respect is contingent on good conduct. The experience of moral dignity is alienable in that one loses it if one conducts oneself in ways that are inimical to the well-being of the community. Moral dignity is connected with conditional respect. Moreover, moral dignity comes in degrees since it depends on moral conduct. This would mean we would not be expected to demonstrate the same respect across human beings, the respect each deserves depends on the 'quantity' of their moral dignity.

We can now proceed to consider Ikuenobe's conception of human rights.

Ikuenobe on Human Rights

Above, we have noted that personhood offers us an African conception of human dignity that serves as the ground for human rights. In his defence of an African approach to human rights, Ikuenobe talks of *substantive human rights* rather than mere human rights as encapsulated in individualistic approaches. According to Ikuenobe, a communitarian approach differs significantly in terms of how it conceptualizes and justifies human rights. Part of unfolding his approach to human rights involves appreciating three crucial interventions he makes in elaborating a communitarian conception of human rights. First, a negative project of rejecting the tendency to ground human dignity on the mere possession of a certain capacity. The second intervention involves appreciating the implications of grounding human rights on a merit-based moral term of personhood or moral dignity. The third intervention involves considering the so-called marginal cases.

Ikuenobe (2023) is very clear regarding the descriptive and evaluative senses of moral dignity. Every human being has factual dignity because they possess ontological capacities. It is this kind of human dignity that is operational in the Universal Declaration of Human Rights. Ikuenobe repudiates the dominant view that factual dignity can ground the universal project of human rights. This view is wrong for him because it is based on a questionable philosophical position. For example, he rejects Metz's friendliness view of human dignity because it grounds it on the capacity for friendliness. It is one thing to recognize the fact that we possess the ontological capacity for friendliness and quite another to associate the capacity for friendliness with intrinsic value. The jump from one to another, argues Ikuenobe, involves an error in reasoning. In fact, he argues "This involves a naturalistic fallacy in that a normative judgment cannot be logically deduced from a factual statement" (2023: 47). For Ikuenobe, the dominant interpretation of human dignity (and the whole debate on moral status) rests on the naturalistic fallacy of ascribing moral value to an ontological feature. For Ikuenobe, capacities are not bearers of intrinsic value.

The second intervention involves rethinking a correct conception of human dignity if is it not based on the mere possession of an ontological capacity, and we should also think about the correct ground for human rights. The normative concept of personhood grounds both the correct view of human dignity and it also serves as the basis for human rights. Human dignity is a function entirely of our development and positive use of our capacities i.e., moral dignity is "meritoriously attained" through the positive use of our capacities (Ikuenobe 2023: 44). Whereas the tendency is to ground human dignity on the mere possession of an ontological capacity, where the human endowment is associated or ascribed with intrinsic value, Ikuenobe interprets the concepts of personhood and/or moral dignity as properly understood as thick concepts. Whereas the intrinsic value associated with human dignity tracks a capacity, thick concepts imagine the integration and interaction of the two to give a different way to think of the value of human dignity. Thick concepts are characterized by both the factual and moral/evaluative components (i.e., the descriptive aspect refers to the mere possession of certain capacities and the moral aspect refers to the actual positive use of these capacities). We can talk of the real value of human dignity in the context of the positive use of the capacities.

The third component involves the element of responsibilities that is crucial in conceptualizing African conceptions of human rights. On a standard account of human rights, they are based on the mere possession of a certain ontological capacity. We have them equally, and they are inalienable. The idea that Ikuenobe invokes to interpret human dignity, personhood, is essentially performance-and-merit-based (i.e., essential to the idea of personhood or moral dignity is that respect accrues towards the moral agent relative to her demonstrating responsibility on social or communal affairs). In fact, Wiredu (2009: 16) observes that "a person would be of a morally sound adult who has demonstrated in practice *a sense of responsibility* to household, lineage and society at large" (see also 1992: 200, emphasis mine). The idea of personhood is intrinsically connected directly with the responsibility that finds expression via other-regarding duties. The connection is of a specific kind, where the moral agent has the responsibility towards her/himself involving the development and proper use of her/his own capacities (Molefe 2019). This is the moral agent's primary responsibility to recognize and positively use her/his capacities (Wiredu 1992). This responsibility extends beyond the individual to embrace the community of which s/he is a member; one must understand her/himself to have a duty to contribute to its well-being.

Notice that moral dignity as a meritorious term exemplifies individuals who have successfully exercised their responsibilities towards the community. How we exercise these duties has implications for moral dignity, human rights and respect. On this view, as much as personhood/moral dignity is conditional on good performance and it is gradational (i.e., comes in degrees), the same holds for human rights. That is, rights are conditional on moral dignity (the more of a person (virtuous we are, the more human rights we have). On this view, human rights track the quality of our use of our ontological capacities. If we fail to use our capacities properly, we lose out on human rights. For example, if we go around killing and raping, we lose out on moral dignity and human rights—society can no longer guarantee peace and safety for such an individual that fails to do good by it (hence, an institution like prisons to deny individuals certain crucial rights). The communitarian conception of human rights, as imagined by Ikuenobe, places a prime on social responsibilities as the basis for imagining the political project of Afro-communitarianism.

We might here ask two important pressing questions. First, how does this system deal with the question of egalitarianism? Second, how does this system accommodate those individuals who cannot use their capacities? Regarding the first question, Molefe (2019, 2022) criticized Ikuenobe's performance-based view for failing to secure moral egalitarianism since it is based on gradational and merit-based concept of moral dignity or personhood. The concept of personhood provides a conditional basis for respect and honour, which will vary from person to person depending on the quality of conduct.

A possible response from Ikuenobe might secure egalitarianism by accounting for it in terms of the community, and not in the concept of a person. Ikuenobe could be construed as basing egalitarianism in the political community, which serves as a platform for the possibility of personhood. Personhood is not the basis for egalitarianism; rather, it is the goal the political community prescribes for the moral patient. The community is a point of departure in the conversation of personhood in African thought. The community has the responsibility to provide resources for every human being to develop their capacities. The basic moral-political insight is that we are equal regarding the opportunities and resources the community provides to ensure conditions for the pursuit and achievement of personhood or moral dignity. The view that Ikuenobe grounds egalitarianism on the community and not on personhood is justified or suggested by him when he talks of "The communal egalitarian spirit" (2017: 449). In another place, he notes that a robust community "exemplify the value of egalitarianism", he proceeds to explain that the egalitarian spirit "requires the *fair* production and distribution of goods and responsibilities so that individuals can experience and live a robust life of dignity" (2023: 54).

On this conception of community-based egalitarianism, it specifies the duties the community has towards its members. Ikuenobe informs us that the community provides "the necessary material conditions for the proper use of human capacities" (2018: 592); "… the material conditions necessary for human well-being" (601); "…the material conditions for its development, proper use …" of capacities (592); "… the material conditions, which make rights or entitlements possible or realizable" (2017: 442). In my interpretation of Ikuenobe's view, egalitarianism is a function of the community (state) equally providing necessary conditions for moral dignity and human rights to be realizable.

Regarding the second question concerning those individuals who cannot use their capacities, I understand Ikuenobe to differentiate between two distinct spheres of human rights. The first sphere refers to the human rights of human beings who cannot use their capacities. For example, we have those human beings who cannot use their capacities because of age (not yet fully developed to use their capacities, e.g., children) or those with moderate/radical disabilities (the so-called marginal cases, e.g., those with serious mental impairments). Moral agents owe those who cannot use their capacities unconditional responsibilities of respect (or, even, human rights). In Ikuenobe's view, the community imposes unconditional responsibilities on moral agents to protect and empower these human beings. The basis for such responsibilities seems to rest on two grounds. The first ground, according to Ikuenobe (2017: 464), is "the moral principle of 'ought implies can". On this principle, it would be unfair and unreasonable to expect this group of persons to pursue moral dignity. The second reason seems to be that moral agents have a responsibility towards this group because it is part of the responsibilities we have to contribute to the collective well-being of the community. We need to take care of these people because they cannot take care of themselves, and we cannot expect them to pursue moral dignity. For those not yet developed like infants and children, we have unconditional responsibilities to create conditions for them to so develop. In this light, even in Ikuenobe's view, we may offer a basket of basic rights that have nothing to do with the positive use of capacities. Even on this view, correctly construed, there are basic sets of human rights we are entitled to, which are necessary to empower those who have not yet reached a point where they can exercise their capacities and protect those who may never be able to develop and use their capacities. The implication seems to be that factual dignity can be a ground for basic human rights to create conditions for the development of our capacities and to protect those whose capacities may never develop.

The second sphere of human rights, proposed by Ikuenobe, is for those human beings who can use their capacities. In this sphere of human rights, we speak of earned human rights in the community. Note Ikuenobe (2018: 592) avers for "those with relevant natural capacities … earning moral personhood is one necessary condition for ascribing rights as social entitlements, which are derived … from one's natural ability to use one's capacities properly". On this view, the positive use of our capacities (which leads to or is tantamount to the acquisition of personhood) is a necessary condition for human rights. Part of what is involved in the acquisition of personhood is the virtuous disposition that is related to promoting the common good. To the extent that we have a character disposition that enhances community, we become entitled to human rights in the community. The exercise of community-building responsibilities associated with personhood is expressive of the prime that Afro-communitarianism places on mutual aid and reciprocity (Wiredu 1992). Whereas human rights, in the typical Euro-American conception of them, tend to generate duties; in the African context, it is the duties inherent in the pursuit and in being a virtuous person that generates and secures human rights. That is, a virtuous moral agent can demand that others should respect him and apportion him the rights due to him because he deserves them. The system at play here is one of reciprocity—one's entitlements are a result of the extent to which they have contributed to human welfare (Cobbah 1987).

On this account, it would seem that rape is a human rights violation in two related ways. On the one hand, one would be failing to nurture their capacities to embody virtue and to promote the common good. In other words, one would be weaponizing their humanity against the ideals of noble humanity as captured by the pursuit and achieving of moral excellence. On the other hand, one would be harming and demeaning the humanity of another. On this view, human rights violations involve acts that deviate from responsibilities to empower humanity, in oneself and in another, to be bearers of virtue, which is the essence of personhood. Human rights violations pivot on deviations from responsibility towards self and others to nurture humanity and community. It involves betraying and undermining the very capacities that should be developed and used to empower humanity.

In short, Ikuenobe articulates a personhood-based account of human rights. Human rights are socio-moral entitlements in the context of the pursuit of virtue (personhood), which in turn enhances communal well-being. On this account, as much as we earn moral dignity through the proper use of our capacities, we also earn human rights. Our human rights are tethered to the positive exercise of our duties towards the community.

Next, I turn to Christopher Allsobrooks' theory of human rights.

Recognition Theory of Human Rights

In several essays, Allsobrook articulates a novel conception of human rights in African philosophy (2018, 2021, 2023). He defends what he describes as the African "recognition-based account of human rights" (2023: 21). He relies on and draws from the wisdom of the tradition of recognition ethical and political theory to contribute to debates on human dignity and human rights in African philosophy (Gauss 2006; Boucher 2011; Martin 2013). He is aware of the weaknesses and criticisms of the recognition school, but he believes that its basic insight regarding the structure of morality and politics is correct. The basic insight of recognition theory is that our customary social practices are the basis for the moral, legal and political enterprises (i.e., right/wrong and human rights emerge from normative customary practices in human cultures). He believes that Gyekye's and Molefe's criticism of Menkiti's conception of a person as the basis for human dignity and human rights misses something crucial about how the concept of personhood implies a common good criterion (human dignity), which is the basis for universal human rights.

In what follows, I will philosophically unfold Allsobrook's conception of human rights. To do so, I will largely rely on his essay 'African Recognition of Dignity as a Basis for Universal Human Rights' (Allsobrook 2023). Three features characterize Allsobrook's account of human rights. First, he rejects the essentialist or naturalist approach to human rights, which grounds them on some special feature of our human nature. Second, he offers his own account of human dignity that is inherent in the normative concept of a person. In this regard, he joins Ikuenobe (2017), Molefe (2020) and Oyowe (2022) in proffering (a Menkiti inspired) personhood-based account of human dignity. Finally, he provides a recognition approach to human rights. I begin with Allsobrook's rejection of naturalism.

Rejection of Naturalism

Human rights, at a meta-ethical level, tend to be grounded either on natural or cultural features (Freeman 1995). The dominant view in the literature in philosophy grounds human rights on some natural feature of our human nature, be it rationality, capabilities, or capacity to care (Kittay 2003; Miller 2017). The idea is that human beings are morally precious—have human dignity—because they possess certain value-endowing capacities. It is in virtue of them possessing these natural attributes that we owe them human rights (Donnelly 1982). In the Euro-American context, the naturalist conception of human dignity and human rights has taken sway. Immanuel Kant, one of the leading modern moral-political thinkers in the Euro-American context, has largely been responsible for the naturalist conception of human dignity and human rights. Most scholars that subscribe to a naturalist conception have posited rationality/autonomy, following Kant, as the basis for human dignity and human rights (see Rosen 2012; Kittay 2003). The same commitment has been an interesting feature of African approaches to human rights.

For example, Gyekye's moderate communitarianism grounds human rights on some natural features of human nature. In some instances, he appears to ground them on possessing the spiritual property of the 'soul' (Gyekye 1992). In some instances, he grounds them on the natural property of rationality/autonomy (Gyekye 1997). In many instances, Kwasi Wiredu grounds human rights on the spiritual property of *okra*, which we may, for a lack of a more accurate concept, associate with the 'soul' (Gyekye 1995). Metz, as we have seen above, grounds them on the natural property of the capacity for friendliness and Motsamai Molefe on the capacity for virtue (or sympathy) (Molefe 2019; Molefe and Muade 2023). Allsobrook, like Ikuenobe, rejects the interpretation of human rights that locates them on some feature of human nature. Two reasons ground his rejection of the naturalist interpretation of human rights.

On the one hand, he seems to agree with Menkiti and Ikuenobe that natural capacities have no value in and of themselves. Allsobrook (alongside Menkiti and Ikuenobe) seem to suggest that reducing human beings and the value associated with them to their psychological capacities misses something crucial and special about Afro-communitarian ethics—the importance of our shared humanity as the basis for human dignity. On the other hand, he proposes that the idea of personhood construed in light of the basic assumptions of recognition theory offers a novel and plausible account of human dignity and human rights, which locates them, in a sense, outside our human nature but in customary practices. Interestingly, Allsobrook grounds human dignity on the African concept of personhood. Below, I turn to his conception of human dignity.

African Personhood and Human Dignity

To approximate Allsobrook's conception of human rights, we must begin by understanding his approach to human dignity. I do so because he grounds human rights on a particular conception of human dignity. I will begin by considering his conception of human dignity. In several places and the essay under consideration here, he is lucid regarding the fact that he derives his account of human dignity from the "recognition of personhood" in Menkiti's adumbrations on it (2023: 20). He argues that the normative concept of a person grounds an African conception of human dignity, which in turn grounds human rights. Remember, for Ikuenobe, at least in my interpretation of his work, the very idea of personhood is equivalent to human dignity (moral dignity). He draws a distinction between factual and moral dignity, and it is the latter that is equivalent to personhood (i.e., to achieve personhood is tantamount to the acquisition of human dignity—the two are the same). To have personhood and/or human dignity is to be virtuous, where the moral agent abounds with other-regarding duties characterized by virtues such as generosity, friendliness, sharing, respect for others, and so on. Below, we will see how these two conceptions of human dignity that associate themselves with Menkiti's adumbrations ultimately differ about the source and content of human dignity.

Like most scholars of African thought, Allsobrook associates personhood with virtue (i.e., a moral agent with a virtuous disposition). To be a person means one's conduct is virtuous, and for Allsobrook, this means one's moral "achievements (in terms of having a virtuous disposition) contribute to the common good" (24). He tethers the notion of personhood as virtue with the notion of the common good. That is, the virtuous moral agent is so because his actions and general conduct are oriented towards promoting the general benefit and good of all (or, the common good). According to him, one cannot be virtuous (or be a person) without first and foremost living according to the standards provided by the community for the sake of contributing to the common good. Secondly, the notion of personhood is not just one of virtue, but it is also essentially one of responsibility or duties towards the promotion of the common good. Hence, we note that one acquires personhood (a virtuous disposition) by aligning with the standards prescribed by the community, and this alignment involves the dispatching of other-regarding duties.

In this view, personhood is characterized as an activity: it is something we do and become in the moral-community context. We become persons as we discharge our duties towards the community, and these are duties that promote the common good. Construing personhood as a virtue has several implications that are crucial for Allsobrook to clarify, particularly if it is to provide a meaningful account of human dignity. First, understanding personhood in terms of the moral language of virtue implies that it embodies a merit-based approach to morality (Darwall 1977). As a merit-based approach, it denotes that morality is a function of the moral agent's performance or conduct in the moral context. At the heart of this merit-based account is the achievement of a good character. If morality is performance-based in the sense of nurturing a good character, it would follow that some individuals would achieve personhood, and some would not (Metz 2010).

Secondly, if personhood embodies a performance-based morality, it will also follow that some moral agents would do better than others, and others would do worse. The idea that personhood is a virtue-and-merit term, would imply that it denotes the kind of value possessed by the agent that comes in degrees: some moral agents would have none (their conduct is poor), low, or high, depending on the quality of conduct (Behrens 2013). The idea that personhood indicates a virtuous disposition of moral agents, which might come in different degrees, depending on the quality of conduct, implies that this moral term is essentially inegalitarian i.e., it is not a term that equalizes moral agents typically associated with human dignity (Molefe 2019, 2022).

The observation that the idea of personhood is not an equalizing moral term is concerning precisely because human dignity is important to ground human rights (Molefe 2019, 2020). If we want everyone to be equally entitled to human rights, we must ground them on the notion of dignity that is equalizing. The notion of a person promulgated by both Allsobrook and Ikuenobe does not seem to be an equalizing moral term. Allsobrook is aware of this problem. He provides a philosophical solution to it. The solution could be appreciated at two levels. First, human dignity, in the relevant sense, is not tantamount to the achievement of personhood itself, as Ikuenobe suggests. He takes a view completely different from the one espoused by Ikuenobe in his interpretation of African personhood. Moral dignity, to use the language used by Ikuenobe to refer to the normative concept of a person, is not the ground for human dignity.

It seems Allsobrook wants us to understand personhood as the final good prescribed by African ethical thought—the idea that the mission or the chief goal of morality is for the moral agent to develop and lead a virtuous life (Wiredu 1992). Human dignity that is to ground an egalitarian and universal franchise of human rights, however, resides elsewhere (i.e., it does not reside in personhood). Instead, personhood as dignified human conduct (virtue) implies a deeper and underlying idea of human dignity. Where exactly does human dignity reside if not on personhood? Allsobrook (like Kwasi Wiredu) makes a critical observation regarding commitment to the idea of a person in African ethical thought that he believes grounds human dignity. Wiredu (2009: 15) remarks as follows regarding personhood, " …to be called a person is to be commended. Inversely, to be called a nonperson is, in general, to be downgraded. But such evaluation presupposes a system of values". He proceeds to inform us that the purview of this system of values spans "the entire sphere of human relations" (ibid.,). Wiredu concludes by noting that the system in question points to "an ethic for a whole society" (ibid.,).

The idea that emerges from Wiredu's comments is that there are two ethical levels of commitment in African ethics. There is a commitment to personhood as the proper goal of a moral life (i.e., the moral agent ought to live a virtuous or dignified life). The commitment to a dignified life (personhood) is grounded on a fundamental and underlying system of values. The underlying system of value is the one that sponsors and justifies the judgement or evaluation whether one is a person or nonperson. It is the system of values underlying the judgement of personhood or lack thereof that Allsobrook posits as the basis for human dignity. In fact, he argues.

> The virtue of such virtuous conduct is that one's achievements contribute to the common good. It is from this communal standard of assessment (and not specifically from the individual's achievement of outstanding moral merit) that we may derive a common good criterion for human rights (2023: 22).

Note that Allsobrook makes a distinction between 'the achievement of outstanding moral merit' (personhood or a dignified life), on the one hand, and 'the communal standard of assessment' that provides the common good criteria. The underlying ethics (the common good) informs and prescribes the final good of personhood as the proper goal of morality. The pursuit of personhood involves both the recognition of the common good and also the responsibility to contribute towards it (the good of all). The common good is the basis for human dignity.

We may construe Allsobrook to be distinguishing two distinct objects of respect (or notions of human dignity). On the one hand, we owe recognition respect to human dignity, which is captured by the common good; and, on the other, we owe appraisal respect to personhood (virtue). It is the former that serves as a criterion for human rights. What exactly does it entail to associate human dignity with the common good? Whereas Allsobrook (alongside Menkiti and Ikuenobe) rejects individualistic and capacity-based conceptions of human dignity, he provides a relational conception of human dignity. On the relational view, to be human is something that we essentially share with others. In fact, he cites Menkiti approvingly on two crucial counts. On the one hand, he cites Menkiti when he jettisons the view that personhood is defined by some intrinsic psychological capacities of our nature; and, on the other, when he avers that "the African conception of the human person is metaphysically communally situated" (cited in Allsobrook, 24). The upshot of this view is that to be human is a feature that we cannot claim to have just as an isolated individual. In fact, it is not possible to be human all alone and all-one—to be human is an essentially and intrinsically relational enterprise—'I am because we are' or 'a person is a person through other persons.'. The emphasis is that everything about us as human beings makes sense because we are a part of a 'we' human community (Ikuenobe 2015). Hence, Allsobrook (29) would opine, "dignity is not an attribute of each single human person, given by nature, but is found in mutual accommodation and mutual respect", which is captured by the idea of the common good.

To exemplify a conception of human dignity as captured by the common good, which points us to the ontological view of being human as caught up with others in inextricable relationships, he gives us examples of struggles against oppression such as slavery. It is in robust human relationships that we thrive as human beings, where we experience dignity. Under conditions of indignity and suffering, human beings tend to engage in struggles to resist and seek to reclaim their human dignity. These struggles against oppression reveal the deep-seated shared humanity, which points us to the common good. This common good is a constant reminder of our shared and connected humanity. Hence, the social practices associated with the pursuit of personhood and the general experience of resisting oppression and indignity point us to the common good, which defines and characterizes human dignity. Human dignity is not what I have as an isolated individual, and it is not an abstract metaphysical thing hanging over me as an individual. Instead, it is a lived reality in human fellowship, which defines, not my humanity as an individual but our humanity, which is experienced ontologically in terms of "beingness-with-others" (Menkiti 2004: 324).

The ethics of the common good is presupposed by both the commitment to personhood and practices of struggles resisting indignity and social injustices. Personhood says we want to live a dignified life (which involves contributing to the common good), and resisting/struggling against indignities/oppression says we must fight against conditions that mar our proper human fellowship. Note how this common good view of human dignity differs from the standard accounts of human dignity we have considered so far in the book.

First, whereas Metz accounts for human dignity strictly in terms of the human capacity for friendliness, this view locates human dignity on our shared human experience of living and belonging to a human community. It is not properties that we have as individuals that define human dignity; it is the collective experience of belonging to the human community and human fellowship and mutuality that captures the common good that embodies our human dignity. Whereas on Metz's account, the moral agent can speak of her own human dignity, on this view we speak only of *our* human dignity. Second, whereas Ikuenobe reduces the concept of human dignity to the achievement of moral personhood, Alsobrooks points us to a deeper and primary ethics that informs personhood as the basis for human dignity (i.e., the common good). Human dignity is best understood when we look at the standards that the community uses to evaluate moral practitioners' achievement of personhood—that standard is the common good. The standard is prior, culturally situated, and it informs the socio-moral aspirations for moral personhood, and hence distinct from it (personhood). It is the standard of the common good that propels us to pursue dignified lives (personhood). It is the standard of the common good that lies underneath a desire for freedom from oppression, indignities, and humiliation. It is this conception of human dignity, as encapsulated by the common good, which grounds human rights.

Next, I turn to Allsobrook's account of human rights.

Recognition Theory of Human Rights

Against the view that human rights are a natural feature of our human nature, Allsobrook defends a non-natural account of human rights. He draws inspiration for his conception of human rights from the recognition school of thought. On this view, human rights, like all moral furniture, are not a part of the natural world. Instead, morality, including human rights, are a construction of human societies to respond to the human condition. The construction of human rights as a response to the human condition takes the form of customary social practices. Human rights as normative social practices emerge in cultural contexts. These social practices are the means for managing and regulating socio-moral human engagements. These habituated forms of social engagements, which Allsobrooks describes as customary practices, become codified into legal norms, or human rights. Three things are worth noting that are crucial to appreciate this account of human rights.

First, we cannot speak of human rights outside of a social or cultural context. Human rights are not prior to human communities; rather, they are posterior to them. Understood in this way, human rights are a contingent feature of human existence. In other words, we might have constructed societies that may have never invented human rights (Feinberg 1970; Donnelly 1982). The contingency of human rights also depends on the kind of society in which they are imagined and invented. In a world free of capitalism and exploitation of workers, we may have had different sets of human rights congruent with the economic model of the society and world. In a world that has never been marred by racism, sexism, and xenophobia, human rights may have taken the shape of this world, if they would emerge at all. The crucial point to notice here is that human rights are created and shaped in the image of the cultures in which they are created. It is for this reason that Allsobrook argues that the current form of international human rights has largely been informed by Euro-American cultures, which makes sense given the economic and political divide of the world between 'developed' and 'developing' countries (2023: 26). This bifurcation of the world is indicative of power relations among nations, cultures and communities, some nations have greater power to influence world political narratives and agendas than others.

Second, human rights in their nature take the form of customary practices. The concept of 'customary' practices reveals something significant about how Allsobrook locates human rights within a recognition school of thought. The recognition school of human rights characterizes them in terms of two features. On the one hand, the "customary behaviour creates rights"; and, on the other hand, "the discursive activity of common law lawyers and international jurists constitutes recognition in the sense of knowing them or formalizing them" (Boucher 2011: 755). The idea that customary practices create rights denotes that they `are inventions of human societies as they attempt to manage socio-political interactions in the attempt to minimize threats to human social existence and to create conducive conditions for human existence. They are described as 'customary' precisely to denote that they are not objective features of our social existence. Each culture, African culture included, has normative social practices, some of which count as human rights. Some of these social practices count as human rights when they are recognized as such. Human rights come into being through what Boucher refers to as the 'discursive activity', which involves the codification or formalization of social practices into human rights. The 'discursive activity' that constitutes human rights, involves the *observation* of social practices, the *identification* of the relevant social practices, and their translation and codification to human rights.

In this view, rape is a human rights violation because it has been recognized and defined so by social recognition and consent. The social recognition of rape has not only been observed to be so by human experience, it has also been codified as so. On this view, remember, the very act of recognition creates human rights. The depth of human experience has come to show us that rape is a human rights violation.

Finally, human rights rest on human dignity. Remember, for Allsobrook, human dignity is the common good criterion, which functions to specify the general good and benefit of every human being in society. Human rights, as social practices, function precisely to fulfil the common good criterion. Allsobrooks (2023: 34) remarks, "a plausible way to account for the universality of human rights is to maintain that they must satisfy the criterion for human dignity, which involves customary normative recognition respect between people". Human dignity, as the common good, points us to our shared humanity in which mutuality and respect are crucial ways of interacting and relating to one another if we are to truly live a fulfilling human life. Human rights are social practices of demonstrating respect for our collective and shared humanity.

Conclusion

This chapter explored three contemporary theories of human rights in African philosophy, namely, the status, personhood, and recognition accounts of human rights. The status view grounds them on the human capacity for friendliness, where human rights serve to protect what is most distinctive about us as human beings. The personhood view conceives of them as socially empowering instruments to ensure a thriving community that supports citizens to acquire personhood. The recognition view conceives of them as social practices that recognize and express respect for our shared humanity and general good as human beings. The first two theories come across as taking a naturalist approach to human rights because ultimately, they ground human dignity and human rights on some feature of our human nature (and our use of some aspects of our nature). However, the status theory of human rights more suitably falls under the naturalist account. The recognition theory takes a non-naturalist interpretation of human rights, where human rights are constructed and social practices designed to express respect for the common good (human dignity). Human dignity is not an individual attribute but is implicit in social practices associated.

References

Allsobrook, C. 2018. Universal Rights from an African Context. In *Perspectives in Social Contract Theory*, 275–319. Washington DC: The Council for Research in Values and Philosophy.

Allsobrook, C. 2021. Recognition of Normative Needs in African Rights. In *Towards an African Philosophy of Needs*, ed. M. Molefe and C. Allsobrook, 187–204. Cham: Palgrave Macmillan.

Allsobrook, C. 2023. African Recognition of Dignity as a Basis for Universal Human Rights. *Acta Academica* 55(1):20–40.

Behrens, K. 2011. *African Philosophy, Thought and Practice and Their Contribution to Environmental Ethics*. Johannesburg: University of Johannesburg.

Behrens, K. 2013. Two 'Normative' Conceptions of Personhood. *Quest: An African Journal of Philosophy* 25(1–2):103–119.

Boucher, D. 2011. The Recognition Theory of Rights. Customary International Law and Human Rights. *Political Studies* 59(3):753–771.

Cobbah, J. 1987. African Values and the Human Rights Debate: An African perspective. *Human Rights Quarterly* 9:309–331.

DeGrazia, D. 2008. Moral Status as a Matter of Degree? *Southern Journal of Philosophy* 46:181–198.

Dladla, N. 2017. Towards an African Critical Philosophy of Race: Ubuntu as a Philo-Praxis of Liberation. *Filosofia Theoretica* 6(1):39–68.

Donnelly, J. 1982. Human Rights and Human Dignity: An Analytic Critique of Non-Western Conceptions of Human Rights. *American Political Science Review* 76:303–316.

Donnelly, J. 2015. Normative Versus Taxonomic Humanity: Varieties of Human Dignity in the Western Tradition. *Journal of Human Rights* 14:1–22.

Darwall, S. 1977. *Two Kinds of Respect. Ethics* 88:36–49.

Feinberg, J. 1970. The Nature and Value of Rights. *The Journal of Value Inquiry* 4:243–257.

Freeman, M. 1995. The Philosophical Foundations of Human Rights. *Human Rights Quarterly* 16:491–514.

Gaus, G. 2006. The Rights Recognition Thesis: Defending and Extending Green. In *Green: Ethics, Metaphysics, and Political Philosophy*, ed. M. Dimova-Cookson and W. J. Mander. Oxford: Oxford University Press.
Gyekye, K. 1992. Person and Community in Akan Thought. In K. Gyekye & K. Wiredu (Eds.), *Ghanaian Philosophical Thought Studies*, vol. 1. Washington, DC: Council for Research in Values and Philosophy, 101–122.
Gyekye, K. 1995. *An Essay on African Philosophical Thought: The Akan Conceptual Scheme*. Temple University Press.
Gyekye, K. 1997. *Tradition and Modernity*. New York: Oxford University Press.
Hughes, G. 2011. The Concept of Dignity in the Universal Declaration of Human Rights. *Journal of Religious Ethics* 39:1–24.
Ikuenobe, P. 2006. *Philosophical Perspectives on Communalism and Morality in African Traditions*. Lanham, MD: Lexington Books.
Ikuenobe, P. 2015. Relational Autonomy, Personhood, and African Traditions. *Philosophy East and West* 65:1005–1029.
Ikuenobe, P. 2016. Good and Beautiful: A Moral-Aesthetic View of Personhood in African Communal Traditions. *Essays in Philosophy* 17:124–163.
Ikuenobe, P. 2017. The Communal Basis for Moral Dignity: An African Perspective. *Philosophical Papers* 45(3):437–469.
Ikuenobe, P. 2018. Human Rights, Personhood, Dignity, and African Communalism. *Journal of Human Rights* 17(5): 589–604.
Ikuenobe, P. 2023. An African Communal Approach to Punishment with Moral Dignity. In *Human Dignity in an African Context*, ed. M. Molefe and C. Allsobrook, 43–65. Switzerland: Palgrave Macmillan.
Jaworska, A., and J. Tannenbaum. 2023. The Grounds of Moral Status. *The Stanford Encyclopedia of Philosophy*. (Spring Edition). Metaphysics Research Lab, Stanford University.
Jones, W., and T. Metz. 2015. The Politics of Philosophy in Africa: A Conversation. *South African Journal of Philosophy* 34(4):538–550.
Kittay, F. 2003. Disability, Equal dignity and Care. Concilium: International. *Journal of Theology* 2:105–115.
Louw, D. 2004. *Ubuntu and the Challenges of Multiculturalism in Post-Apartheid South Africa*. Utrecht: Centre for Southern Africa.
Martin, R. 2013. Human Rights and the Social Recognition Thesis. *Journal of Social Philosophy* 44(1): 1–21.
McNaughton, D., and P. Rawling. 1992. Honoring and Promoting Values. *Ethics* 102 (4): 835–843.
Menkiti, I. 1984. Person and Community in African Traditional Thought. In *African philosophy: an introduction*, ed. R. Wright. Lanham, MD: University Press of America.
Menkiti, I. 2004. On the Normative Conception of a Person. In *A Companion to African Philosophy*, ed. K. Wiredu. Oxford: Blackwell.
Metz, T. 2007a. Toward an African Moral Theory. *The Journal of Political Philosophy* 15:321–341.
Metz, T. 2007b. Ubuntu as a Moral Theory: Reply to Four Critics. *South African Journal of Philosophy= Suid-Afrikaanse Tydskrif vir Wysbegeerte* 26(4): 369–387.
Metz, T. 2010. Human Dignity, Capital Punishment and an African Moral Theory: Toward a New Philosophy of Human Rights. *Journal of Human Rights* 9:81–99.
Metz, T. 2011. Ubuntu as a Moral Theory and Human Rights in South Africa. *African Human Rights Law Journal* 11(2): 532–559.
Metz, T. 2012a. African Conceptions of Human Dignity: Vitality and Community as the Ground of Human Rights. *Human Rights Review* 13:19–37.
Metz, T. 2012b. An African Theory of Moral Status: A Relational Alternative to Individualism and Holism. *Ethical Theory and Moral Practice: An International Forum* 14:387–402.
Metz, T. 2013. Two Conceptions of African Ethics in the Work of D. A. Masolo. *Quest* 25:7–15.
Metz, T. 2014. The Western Ethic of Care or an Afro-communitarian Ethic? Specifying the Right Relational Morality. *Journal of Global Ethics* 9(1): 77–92.

Metz, T. 2016. An Ubuntu-based Evaluation of the South African State's Responses to Marikana: Where's the Reconciliation? *Politikon* 44(2):287–303.
Metz, T. 2022. *A Relational Moral Theory: African Ethics in and Beyond the Continent*. Oxford: Oxford University Press.
Miller, S. 2017. Reconsidering Dignity Relationally. *Ethics and Social Welfare* 11:108–121.
Mkhize, N. 2008. Ubuntu and Harmony, An African Approach to Morality and Ethics. In *Person in Community, African Ethics in a Global Culture*, ed. Ronald Nicolson, 35–44. Scottsville: University of Kwa-Zulu Natal Press.
Molefe, M. (2017). A Critique of Thad Metz's African Theory of Moral Status. *South African Journal of Philosophy* 36:195–205.
Molefe, M. 2019. *An African Philosophy of Personhood, Morality and Politics*. New York, NY: Palgrave Macmillan.
Molefe, M. 2020. *An African Ethics of Personhood and Bioethics: A Reflection on Abortion and Euthanasia*. New York: Palgrave Macmillan.
Molefe, M. 2022. *Human Dignity in African Philosophy: A Very Short Introduction*. New York: Springer.
Molefe, M. 2024. African, Black, and Western Conceptions of Human Dignity. *The Monist* 107(3):237–250.
Molefe, M., and E. Maude. 2023. An Appraisal of "African Perspectives of Moral Status: A Framework for Evaluating Global Bioethical Issues". *Arụmarụka: Journal of Conversational Thinking* 3(1): 25–50.
Nkondo, G. 2007. Ubuntu as a Public Policy in South Africa: A Conceptual Framework. *International Journal of African Renaissance Studies* 2:88–100.
Oyowe, A. 2013. Personhood and Social Power in African Thought. *Alternation* 20:203–228.
Oyowe, O. A. 2022. *Menkiti's Moral Man*. Bloomsbury Publishing PLC.
Ramose, M. 1999. *African Philosophy Through Ubuntu*. Harare: Mond Books.
Reichlin, M. 2014. Moral Status. In *Encyclopedia of Global Bioethics*, ed. H. ten Have. Cham: Springer.
Rosen, M. 2012. *Dignity: Its History and Meaning*. Cambridge, MA: Harvard University Press.
Shutte, A. 2001. *Ubuntu: An Ethic for a New South Africa*. Pietermaritzburg: Cluster Publications.
Sulmasy, D. 2008. Dignity and Bioethics: History, Theory, and Selected Applications. In *The President's Council on Bioethics, Human Dignity and Bioethics: Essays Commissioned by the President's Council*, 469–501. Washington, DC: President's Council on Bioethics.
Toscano, M. 2011. Human Dignity as High Moral Status. *The Ethics Forum* 6:4–25.
Tutu, D. 1999. *No Future Without Forgiveness*. New York: Random House.
Waldron, J. 2012. Dignity and Rank. *Archives Européenes de Sociologie* 48:201–237.
Wiredu, K. 1992. Moral Foundations of an African Culture. In *Person and Community: Ghanaian Philosophical Studies, 1*, ed. K. Wiredu and K. Gyekye, 192–206. Washington, DC: The Council for Research in Values and Philosophy.
Wiredu, K. 2009. An Oral Philosophy of Personhood: Comments on Philosophy and Orality. *Research in African Literatures* 40(1): 8–18.
Verhoef, H., and C. Michel. 1997. Studying Morality Within the African Context: A Model of Moral Analysis and Construction. *Journal of Moral Education* 26:389–407.

Chapter 4
Conclusion

This chapter provides overall and concluding remarks on some of the issues covered in the book. It does so in two ways. On the one hand, I revisit some of the major concepts and debates on human rights in African philosophy. On the other hand, I will indicate ways in which future research might advance the discourse on human rights in African philosophy. In what follows, I will traverse four specific themes as a way to bring this chapter to a close (a) the debate on the concept of personhood, (b) the debate on human dignity; (c) reflections on the concept and place of human rights in African thought and d) skepticism regarding human rights.

The Debate on Personhood

One of the outstanding issues regarding personhood in African thought revolves around which concept of it is suitable to ground human rights. Notice, we can differentiate between two distinct normative concepts of a person. The one moral concept is capacity-based, and the literature in philosophy describes this notion in terms of moral status (Behrens 2013). Another concept is action-based in as far as it revolves around the quality of human conduct. Kevin Behrens (2013) makes a similar distinction in terms of the *patient-centred* and *agent-centred* notions of a person. The patient-centred notion assigns value to a human being relative to whether s/he possesses the relevant ontological capacity. That is, if for example rationality is the basis for moral status, all human beings that possess this capacity do have moral status (or, even human dignity). It is the mere possession of moral status that assigns intrinsic value (or moral worth) to the being under consideration. On the other hand, the agent-centred notion assigns it on the basis of the quality of human conduct, excellence or virtue.

Among classical theories of human rights, Menkiti appears to ground the entire moral-political project on the agent-centred notion of a person—the maximalist

M. Molefe, *An Introduction to Human Rights in African Philosophy*, SpringerBriefs in Ethics, https://doi.org/10.1007/978-3-032-04447-1_4

conception of a person. He denies that capacities can serve as a ground for personhood. Personhood is not what we are born with, rather it is what we achieve in the moral-political context. For Menkiti, for example, the ideas of human dignity and human rights "… go beyond the raw appetitive level to the special level marked by the dignity of the person, something more would seem to be needed". The more he has is mind is a life-ling project committed to the "ingathering of excellences" of character. Social justice revolves around the state's responsibilities towards empowering its citizens to successfully prue human dignity, and citizens also have (other-regarding) duties towards to empower another to be and to do better. These duties revolve around the political ideal and goal of promoting the communal well-being. Menkiti's preference of the normative concept of a person that places an emphasis on our duties to promote the common is the very reason why human rights secondary. Rights come second to social duties because they tend not to be common good oriented in the way duties associated with personhood tend to be self-centred in a way that may threaten the collective conscious and empathy central in Afro-communitarianism.

Scholars like Ikuenobe and Allsobrook in the contemporary debates on human rights tend to follow Menkiti's approach of grounding human rights on the agent-centred notion of a person, albeit differently. For example, Ikuenobe grounds human dignity and human rights on the merit-based concept of a person. On this view, as much as we earn moral dignity, we also earn human rights. The consequence of rights being earned on this view is not surprising at all precisely because Ikuenobe basis them on a concept of virtue, which we merit relative to the quality of our disposition and conduct. Allsobrook also grounds human rights on the normative concept of personhood (virtue). What is distinctive about his approach is that it is not exactly personhood that grounds human rights, but the underlying concept of the common good that specifies the standard of assessment for it (personhood or a dignified life). Moral agents are judged to be living a dignified life (virtuous life) on the basis of the standard of assessment of the common good. Though the concept of a person itself is a merit term, the standard of assessment (the common good) is not a merit-based, it is one that equally specifies the standard of excellence and decency that the state and human beings must live up to.

Moderate communitarianism imagines a political theory that is grounded on both the patient-and-agent-centred notions of a person. The patient-centered notion grounds moral status or human dignity on the capacity for autonomy (in other instances it also invokes religious interpretations of it such as *imago dei*). The patient-centred aspect of this moral theory grounds, on the main, negative human rights, which imposes duties on the state and members of society not to interfere and harm bearers of human dignity. The agent-centred aspect recognizes the relational nature of being human, and it tethers it to the social duties to promote the common good. Our relational nature orients us to connect with others and it equally imposes duties on us to empower them. The friendliness view of human rights, on the other hand, entirely relies on the patient-centred notion of a person to account for social social justice. We have human rights because we have the capacity for friendliness, whether as subjects or objects of such a way of relating. This capacity is both necessary and sufficient for human rights.

The above analysis indicates three salient approaches on the relationship between personhood and human rights in African philosophy. Some theories adopt the agent-centred theory of a person as the ground for human rights. Some theories adopt the patient-centred approach—the idea of moral status that tends to be dominant in the Euro-American literature, to ground human rights. Finally, we have moderate communitarianism that espouses both the patient-and-agent-centred approaches to imagine a robust political theory. Ultimately, however, moderate communitarianism grounds human rights on the capacity for autonomy.

There is something particularly attractive about a moral-political system that places duties and responsibility on the front sit. If we think of duties as the needs-based service that we owe to our fellow human beings then radical communitarianism imagines a political community, or the state and its citizens, that relate to each as bearers of duties that seek to recognize and resp[ect our humanity by responding to the human condition of need, and moreover that appreciates that value of our shared humanity that we experience in a community with other human beings. Whereas this duty-based political orientation is attractive inasfar as it requires us to respond to the human condition, it is plagued two related concerns.

On the one hand, radical communitarianism does not seem to appreciate the complexity associated with the scarcity of the human will or courage, institutionally or individually, to act motivated by duty to respond to human needs. The scarcity of such duty-motivated state or individuals is a common feature of human experience. The corruption and looting of state coffers to feed human greed while flagrantly ignoring human need is a common occurrence. We want a political system that can secure human needs and create avenues that can challenge such a state. Human rights seem to be a powerful tool to empower individuals and remedy such conditions. I am not sure if rights will be powerful enough in a context where they are outrightly declared to be secondary.

On the other hand, it is not entirely clear how radical communitarianism can function in complex contexts characterized by scarcity and competition over resources. Above we consider scarcity of a character associated with a duty-based politics, now we consider a duty-based political system that has to adjudicate and distribute scarce resources over which there competing or even conflicting interests, as characterized by a Siamese crocodile that has a single stomach and two heads. How do we fairly and equally distribute the common good in the context of the political system of duties—the idea of a collective good, as understood in radical communitarianism, can be a very burdensome one. Rights, at a prima facie level, seem to be suitable to navigate pricisely the kinds of conflicts and competition associated with scarcity in a way that a collective oriented political system is not. It occurs to me that it is much more complex, in a legal context, ro adjudicate over conflicts on the basis of rights than on the duties based on care. There is regularity and fixedness associated with rights, which is not typical in care-based duties that respond to human needs. The power of the pull of the demand associated with a right-holder seems to be greater when compared to a pull of a need-based duty, the former functions at the level of entitlement and another on the basis of a quality of the character of the duty bearer.

On the face of it, moderate communitarianism wants to go a bit further than radical communitarianism in terms of elevating the place of human rights in African political thought. Whereas Afro-communitarianism has generally not been able to carve out a clear parameter for the individual and individuality, moderate communitarianism correctrs this defect by emphasizing the individualistic features that must be central in moral-political thought. Borrowing from the Kantian idea of autonomy, he insists on a political theory that includes the individual, the value associated with the individual (human dignity), and the rights that serve to protect and enhance the value of the individual, all the while cognizant of importance of the community. There is something attractive about the idea that there are projects and activities that have to do with the individual, and the political community has a right to protect these. Gyekye imagines that culturally, a society may frown upon homosexuality, that must not however be a sufficient ground to deny the individual the right to determine heer own sexuality and how to express it inspite of the cultural community frowning upon it.

Whilst Gyekye's moderate communitarianism attempts to accommodate individuality, human dignity and human rights is admirable, it is plagues by serious concerns. On the one hand, Gyekye's espousal of anti-supererogation negates his attempt to carve out a place for the individual and her own projects in moral and political philosophy. Anti-supererogation is the idea that the scope of our duties have no limits, as long as there is a duty before, it is our responsibility to fulfil it. The implication is that the individual will be so burdened by the collective duties towards the community to a point of threatening individuality, or presenting prospects of a less than robust individual. On the other hand, Gyekye's moderate communitarian argument that in a context of a conflict between duties associated with the common good and human rights, the former ought to prevail over the latter threatens the very *moderation* promised by his political theory. Anti-supererogation and the secondarization of human rights appears to really threaten the value of human rights in moderate communitarianism.

I turn now to debates on human dignity.

Debates on Human Dignity

The idea of human dignity is central to the debates on human rights in philosophy. It is only recently that the idea of human dignity is gaining some real traction in the literature in African philosophy (Metz 2012, 2024; Molefe 2019, 2022, 2024; Molefe and Allsobrook 2023; Molefe and Muade 2023). The notion of human dignity features in both the classical and contemporary theories of human rights in African philosophy. In the context of classical theories of human rights, the idea of human dignity did not feature significantly as an object of philosophical engagement. Both Menkiti and Gyekye are aware of this concept, its importance in ethical theory, but they never quite made it the focus of their philosophical inquiry drawing from African resources. Both these scholars never even define how they understand this concept. They seem content to operate on the level of intuition and assumption that we are all aware of it.

Outstanding feature of Menkiti's approach to human dignity characteristically repudiates the idea that it is a function entirely of merely possessing some ontological feature or capacity. For him, it would seem that our ontological capacities, at best, they are either morally neutral or instrumentally valuable. Menkiti appears to reduce human dignity to the acquisition of virtue, or moral personhood.[1] Gyekye, on the other hand, criticizes Menkiti precisely because his view fails to recognize the outstanding individual feature of our nature (i.e., the capacity for autonomy that grounds human rights) that grounds human dignity. Gyekye variously invokes autonomy and/or *imago die*, as possible theories of human dignity to bolster his account of human rights in African thought.

Both these scholars could have better in their engagement with the idea of human dignity to advance scholarship. Menkiti and Ikuenobe, for example, would have done well to provide details of how the maximamlist concept captures human dignity, and how his conception is more compelling than the conventional approach to human dignity in the literature that tends to reduce it to distinctive capacities of our human nature (Behrens 2013). Gyekye, on his part, invokes the idea of human dignity because it grounds human rights. Where he fails to advance African moral-theorisation is that he relies entirely on the Euro-American conceptions of human dignity to bolster his political theory. He does well to argue that a robust understanding of African thought ought to recognize the individualistic features, which secures the relevance and importance of human dignity (and human rights). When he is supposed to provide his account of human dignity, he invokes Kant's account of it that basis it on autonomy and/or the Christian view of *imago dei*. We might charitably interpret Gyekye's borrowing from Euro-American conception of human dignity because priority might have been to indicate to African readers that we may not simply dismiss the crucial universal concept of human dignity in African political thought. This charitable interpretation, however, does not erase his philosophical debt, following his own style of doing philosophy, where he usually draws from indigenous intellectual and axiological heritage as the basis for his moderate communitarianism.

In the contemporary theories, we see a deliberate attempt to advance the literature regarding theorizing about human dignity in African philosophy. Scholars such as Metz (2011, 2012, 2024; Oyowe, 2013, 2022; Ikuenobe 2018; Molefe, 2019, 2024; Molefe and Allsobrook 2023) develop their own theories of human dignity with an African pedigree. Thaddeus Metz defends the view that we have moral

[1] In his latter writings, he seems to now accept the idea that human beings, in and of themselves, are intrinsically valuable. Note this comment by Menkiti, "The individual counts and is ultimately the bearer of intrinsic value". On this latter rendition, it would seem that some individual features of our human nature serve as the basis of our human dignity, which view is different from his initial view.

worth because we have the special social abilities—the capacity for friendliness, which includes both being friendly and being treated that way. We have human rights because of this crucial feature of our human nature. Ikuenobe and Allsobrook pursue conceptions of human dignity that pivot on the agent-centred notion of a person—the normative concept of a person. Ikuenobe merely rejects approaches that accounts for human dignity in terms of merely possessing a certain ontological capacity; he associates our capacities with instrumental value. Instead, he argues that the nurturing and the positive use of our capacities is the basis for human dignity. Human dignity is something that we achieve by exercising our responsibility to promote to communal well-being. Whereas Metz's view of human dignity considers it to be unconditional and inalienable feature of our nature, Ikuenobe's view considers it to be conditional and alienable depending on our conduct.

On his part, Allsobrook grounds human dignity on the norms we use to assess some agent to have achieved personhood, and not personhood itself. On his account, we can derive the view of human dignity on the norms we use to apportion or deny personhood to a moral agent. What African culture prescribes as rituals, practices and standards for personhood and excellence are indicative of the underlying criterion of human dignity. Like Ikuenobe, he derives or associates human dignity with the agent-centred notion of person. Unlike Ikuenobe, it is not the actual achievement of personhood that secures human dignity, but the judgement that one is a person points us to the common good standard that serves as a standard for assessing moral excellence. Unlike Metz and Ikuenobe, Allsobrook regards human dignity in Afro-communitarian to be a possession, not of an individual, but something we have in our collective and shared humanity. We have human in and between ourselves as human beings.

The idea of human dignity is typically crucial to ground egalitarianism in political theory (Rosen 2012). In the literature in moral-political philosophy, we are equal because we possess a certain equalizing ontological capacity. The theories of human dignity we have explored in this book provide us with different ways to conceptualize socio-political egalitarianism. Metz's theory would secure our equality on the basis of our capacity for friendliness. We are equal merely because we possess the relevant capacity. We may possess this capacity for friendliness in differing measures, but equality is secured strictly by merely possessing the relevant capacity to an sufficient threshold level. On Metz's view, for example, babies do have moral status, but lack human dignity because as much as they can be objects of friendly relations, they cannot be subjects of such relationships—human dignity is a function of both being an object and subject of friendly relations.

At face value, Ikuenobe's performance-based conception of human dignity fails to provide egalitarianism because it basis it on a term that at its core is inegalitarian since personhood is something that we achieve and comes in degrees. I suggested probably egalitarianism for Ikuenobe's view is a function of the resources the community owes to moral agents for them to nurture and positively use their capacities in pursuit of personhood and the common good, and the capacities themselves. We are equal insofar as we all require assistance and empowerment for the community (or the state) to develop and function. The commitment to personhood is justified by the initial egalitarianism underlying Afro-communitarianism. I also suspect that Allsobrook's conception of egalitarianism resides in the standard of the common good that informs and justifies our commitment to egalitarianism. It would seem that Ikuenobe's and Allsobrook's vision of social egalitarianism may be very similar to each other—the commitment to the common good is the standard for egalitarianism.

Major take away from the contemnporary theories of human dignity. There is something absolutely fascinating about capacity-based theories of human dignity—the fact that what makes us morally special is the kind of a thing that we are. Human dignity is not something that we achieve or earn. The basis for why states and fellow citizens must respect us is merely the fact that we possess the relevant value-endowing capacities (e.g., the capacity for friendliness). It provides a straightforward way to secure egalitarianism, one simply has to possess the relevant ontological features. The difficulty, however, with this view comes in two ways. On the one hand, it is difficult to identify and justify the relevant value-endowing property. On the other hand, this approach seems not to mind the is-ought gap—the idea that we cannot derive a value from a fact (Ikuenobe 2018). What makes the mere fact that we possess a particular ontological feature makes us to have moral worth?

The views like that of Ikuenobe and Allsobrook given their emphasis on the idea of moral achievement tethered to the common as the basis for human dignity are able to capture the distinctive feature of Afro-communitarian political theory—the importance of social responsibility in politics. Politics is a zone for exercising institutional resources and power to respond to human needs to secure the common good. Several issues, however, challenge this view. What happens in the context of scarcity of resources to secure the common good? It is difficult to pin down the content of the common good that all scholars can agree on. Scholars of African thought often eschew providing the content of such goods. In a context of the history of oppression, one wonders if the capacity-based approach would not serve a better approach to the issue of egalitarianism.

The Place and Relevance of the Concept of Human Right in African Philosophy

Do human rights truly have a place in Afro-communitarianism? Jack Donnelly (1982) in his exposition of the non-Euro-American cultures had observed that they did not appear to have a concept of a right as a centrally governing political resource in imagining social organization and justice. He distinguishes between a right action and right as an entitlement (Donnelly 2009). A right is an entitlement against the state (and others) in society, which also creates duties for them (either positive or negative). He observes that non-Euro-American societies operate largely by appealing to social duties, as we have seen in Menkiti's, Gyekye's, Ikuenobe's adumbrations. Whereas rights fundamentally pivot on what others owe to us, the social duties underpinning Afro-communitarianism tend to pivot on what we owe towards others (see Molefe 2018). Human rights tend to have an essentially self-regarding element, whereas duties an other-regarding one. Joel Feinberg captures the essential self-centred focus and power of human rights in a very revealing fashion.

In the essay 'The Nature and Value of Human Rights', Feinberg (1970) makes a profound argument concerning the nature of human rights. He structures his argument around a thought experiment that imagines a community called Nowheresville. Nowheresville is like our (think here of Euro-American) society like every other society except that it has no rights. He sets up this thought experiment to demonstrate that a society without rights lacks something very crucial. Feinberg (1970: 249) observes that "The most conspicuous difference, I think, between the Nowheresvillians and ourselves has something to do with the activity of claiming". A distinctive feature of human rights is the empowerment it affords moral agents, or citizens, to make claims against their governments. Feinberg (1970: 252, emphasis mine) argues,

> … that their [human rights] characteristic use and that for which they are distinctively well suited, is to be *claimed, demanded, affirmed, insisted* upon. They are especially sturdy objects to "stand upon," a most useful sort of moral furniture. Having rights, of course, makes claiming possible; but *it is claiming that gives rights their special moral significance*.

According to Feinberg rights are really powerful things to have in the world. They really empower the moral agent or citizen against the state and society at large. It is important to underscore the idea that human rights are not a favor or a request. Human rights operate at a completely different level. Human rights are essentially definable in terms of the activity of claiming i.e., one that has human rights, if they are rights at all, denotes that they are in a position to claim and that activity of claiming is legitimate practive of a right-holder. The activity of claiming definitive of rights, Feinberg argues, involves making demands and insisting on what is due to the right-holder. A position of the right-holder is a very powerful one.

The association of human rights with the activity of claiming as something that we can demand or insist upon calls to mind the idea of rights as trumps. The idea of rights as trumps signifies the importance and seriousness of human rights in social organization and social justice particularly when they are pitted against non-rights based normative considerations. The idea of human rights as trumps indicates their peremptory status, which means that "(t)he reasons that rights provide are particularly powerful or weighty reasons, which override reasons of other sorts" (Wenar 2023: n.p). The idea is that human rights, when ranked with non-rights considerations, take special consideration or priority, all things being equal. The individual human right may be so powerful to prevent a building project that might require her/his private property to be moved elsewhere for the benefit of the community. We should not, however, overstate the normative priority of human rights to imply that they are absolute. In fact, scholars considers them to be queit stringent, but not necessarily absolute (Donnelly 1982). That implies that all things being equal, human rights prevail over non-rights considerations, but when things are not equal, rights may be set aside. In very rare and exceptional occasions, we may override human rights, perhaps in favour of group rights on occasion.

Above I have made two observations. First, I observed that African cultures tend to be duty-based. Second, I have given us a picture of human rights as peremptory claims that are normatively superior to non-rights requirements. I have raised these two issues to reflect on the status and place of human rights in African philosophy, particularly given the legacy and impact of the idea similar to that of Menkiti, Gyekye and Ikuenobe. For starters, Menkiti was the first to observe that human rights do feature in African thought, but they tend only to enjoy the secondary status. Gyekye vehemently argues for the relevance and importance of human rights in African philosophy to a point of considering them equal with duties. What is curious about hiw view, however, are the claims he makes about human rights. Gyekye and Wiredu (1992: 115) is unequivocal that "communitarianism cannot be expected to make a fetish of rights". He proceeds to observe that Afro-communitarianism cannot be expected to place "rights at the front burner of its concerns and preoccupations" (ibid.,).

Finally, he observes that in the case that a rights-based consideration clashes with some of the objectives of the community (which are related to promoting the common good), the duties should take priority over rights. Gyekye is also clear that it is not allowed for individuals to be insisting on their rights when confronted with the common good. Ikuenobe (2018: 594) also makes similar observation regarding the status of human rights against social duties, he argues that for the "*priority (based on practical reason) of duty over rights*". One question arises regarding this treatment of human rights in African philosophy. Are we dealing with human rights as they feature in the Euro-American political cultures?

The view that scholars from African scholars seems to be that rights are important as they reflect the individuality of persons. The individuality of persons, however, is not exhausted by human rights. In fact, the stronger argument seems to be that the priority of duties functions precisely to protect human rights. The very goals and considerations motivating individuals to insist on their rights are already comprehended on social goals associated with human dignity. The reason why individuals should not insist on them is twofold. On the one hand, the activity of claiming may be inimical to the sense of community, human fellowship and brotherhood essential in communitarianism. The moral psychology of claiming individuates and places the interests of the individual against those of the community. Secondly, the substance of duties associated with the good functions precisely to empower and address concerns that rights are attempting to solve. The social duties do so in a way that foster community and humanity. Hence, it may be otiose to insist on one's rights when the community already provides for their substance via social duties. Does this mean Donnelly (1982) was correct to observe that Afro-communitarianism functions at a level of duties and not rights (see Oyowe 2013, 2014).

We may also ask—can we meaningfully speak of human rights if they are merely secondary? We may also proceed to inquire whether we have a proper sense of human rights when they are regarded as the kinds of things that we can set aside for the sake of the common good. If we strip them of their power that is associated with the activity of claiming, demanding and insisting, why do we want to claim that there are important in African political thought. Furthermore, if they are now the kind of a thing that we earn, wherein are they special and distinctive to protect and empower the individual. The difficult and lingering question is: what is special about having human rights in Afro-communitarianism as imagined by Menkiti and Gyekye if they are secondary to duties? And, what is special about human rights, according to Ikuenobe, if they are merited and achieved as opposed to inherent to something about human nature?

Skepticism Regarding Human Rights in African Political Thought

Another crucial aspect that did feature (but suggested in the book) is the skepticism towards human rights. We can identify at least three leading positions on human rights in African philosophy. First, we have the view associated with radical communitarianism that assigns human rights a secondary status. The personhood view may be categorized under the first view. Secondly, we have the view that considers rights to be a central feature of human rights in African philosophy. This view is represented by moderate communitarianism and scholars such as Metz that defends friendliness view of human rights. Finally, we have the view that considers rights to be foreign in African cultures and thought. On this view, human rights are not a natural part of African political thought. On this view, human rights are diametrically opposed to to the Afro-communitarianism moral-political orientation.

Several reasons have been proffered to sponsor the view that rejects human rights in African thought. First, the individualism that is a hallmark of human rights is foreign to the African cultures and axiological orientation. Whereas Afro-communitarianism tends to place a prime on the community, harmony and social duties, human rights tends to focus on the individual and the duties they create for others towards individual. The emphasis on the former view is on the collective good and the emphasis on the latter is on the individual good (Ake 1987). Secondly, the language and practice of entitlements, associated with human rights, deviates from the language associated with the pursuit of personhood (virtue) and/or *ubuntu*. The language of human rights tends to be imagine an adversarial relationship, where one claims rights *against* others, whereas the language of Afro-communitarianism tends to emphasise what we owe to one another—I am because we are (Molefe 2017). The political culture and imagination characteristic of African thought is much closer to the ideas in Avishai Margalit (2005) book *The Decent Society*, which considers the language of humiliation and its opposite honour as central in political thought. A decent society is one that does not humiliate its citizens. We may understand humiliation to involve a use of state power to undermine human dignity. The goal of a state and its citizens is to empower citizens to live a life of honour, to use the parlance of African cultures, personhood or *ubuntu*.

The similarity between Margalit's ideas and Afro-communitarianism is important because it captures two crucial facets of Afro-communitarian thought. It recognizes the centrality of human dignity in African political thought. It also captures the importance of the idea of honour that is expressed via a culture of duties to promote to common good. The similarity, however, only goes so far. Another crucial and positive aspect of this skepticism that responds directly to the individualism of the idea of human rights is what scholars and policy makers in Africa describe as *people's rights* or *collective rights*. This comment by Claude Ake (1987: 9, emphasis mine) elucidates the idea of collective rights,

> It is necessary to extend the idea of human rights to include *collective human rights for corporate social groups such as the family, the lineage, the ethnic group*. Our people still think large-ly in terms of collective rights and express their commitment to it constantly in their behaviour. This disposition underlies the zeal for community develop-ment and the enormous sacrifices which poor people readily make

The idea of collective rights that tend towards community development are enshrined the *African Charter on Human Rights and People's Rights*, which was adopted by the Organization of African Unity. The idea of people's rights captures another under-explored facet of human rights in philosophy in general. We hope scholars will start paying attention to this idea of collective human rights.

References

Ake, C. 1987. The African Context of Human Rights. *Africa Today* 34:5–12.

Behrens, K. 2013. Two 'Normative' Conceptions of Personhood. *Quest: An African Journal of Philosophy* 25:103–119.

Donnelly, J. 1982. Human Rights as Natural Rights. *Human Rights Quarterly* 4:391–405.

Donnely, J. 2009. *Human Dignity and Human Rights*. Denver: Josef Korbel School of International Studies.

Feinberg, J. 1970. The Nature and Value of Rights. *Journal Value Inquiry* 4:243–260.

Gyekye, K., and K. Wiredu, eds. 1992. *Person and Community: Ghanaian Philosophical Studies, 1*. Washington, DC: Council for Research in Values and Philosophy.

Ikuenobe, P. 2018. Human Rights, Personhood, Dignity, and African Communalism. *Journal of Human Rights* 17:589–604.

Margalit, A. 2005. Political Theology: The Authority of God. *Theoria* 52(106): 37–50.

Metz, T. 2011. Ubuntu as a Moral Theory and Human Rights in South Africa. *African Human Rights Law Journal* 11:532–559.

Metz, T. 2012. African Conceptions of Human Dignity: Vitality and Community as the Ground of Human Rights. *Human Rights Review (Piscataway, NJ)* 1 (13): 19–37.

Metz, T. 2024. A Relational Theory of Dignity and Human Rights: An Alternative to Autonomy. *The Monist* 107(3):211–224.

Molefe, M. 2017. Personhood and Rights in an African Tradition. *Politikon* 45:217–231.

Molefe, M. 2018. Personhood and Rights in an African Tradition. *Politikon* 45(2): 217–231.

Molefe, M. 2019. *An African Philosophy of Personhood, Morality and Politics*. New York, NY: Palgrave Macmillan.

Molefe, M. 2022. *Human Dignity in Africa: A Very Short Introduction*. Cham: Springer.

Molefe, M. 2024. African, Black, and Western Conceptions of Human Dignity. *The Monist* 107(3): 237–250.

Molefe, M., and C. Allsobrook. 2023. *Human Dignity in an African Context*. New York: Macmillan Palgrave.

Molefe, M., & Muade, E. 2023. *African Ethics and Death: Moral Status and Human Dignity in Ubuntu Thinking*. Routledge.

Oyowe, O. A. 2013. Personhood and Social Power in African Thought. *Alternation* 20(1): 203–228.

Oyowe, O. A. 2014. An African Conception of Human Rights? Comments on the Challenges of Relativism. *Human Rights Review* 15(3):329–347.

Oyowe, O.A. 2022. *Menkiti's Moral Man*. Bloomsbury Publishing PLC.

Rosen, M. 2012. *Dignity: Its History and Meaning*. Cambridge, MA: Harvard University Press.

Wenar, L. 2023. Rights. In The Stanford Encyclopedia of Philosophy (Spring 2023 Edition), ed. Edward N. Zalta & Uri Nodelman. https://plato.stanford.edu/archives/spr2023/entries/rights/.

Index

M. Molefe, *An Introduction to Human Rights in African Philosophy*, SpringerBriefs in Ethics, https://doi.org/10.1007/978-3-032-04447-1

GPSR Compliance
The European Union's (EU) General Product Safety Regulation (GPSR) is a set of rules that requires consumer products to be safe and our obligations to ensure this.

If you have any concerns about our products, you can contact us on

ProductSafety@springernature.com

In case Publisher is established outside the EU, the EU authorized representative is:

Springer Nature Customer Service Center GmbH
Europaplatz 3
69115 Heidelberg, Germany

www.ingramcontent.com/pod-product-compliance
Lightning Source LLC
Chambersburg PA
CBHW070751121125
35217CB00020B/111
9783032044464